# Corrigenda

Page 10; Map. Reverse the captions for Creux Harbour granite and Sark Quartz-biotite.
Page 17; para 1, line 16; change 'Vazon Bay Hotel and golf' to read 'La Grande Mare Country'; para 3. Delete; "with the Trepied Dolmen on the small hillock behind it".
Page 27; para. 2. Delete the sentence beginning 'These are presumably'.
Page 33; Lower picture; for 'Dolerite read 'Lamprophyte'. (The dolerite vein is about 15m south of this)
Page 51; para 2, line 2; delete 'a huge' and substitute 'an'.
Page 63; The Bryophytes, line 2; change 'the mainland' to read 'Britain'.
Page 72; para 5, line 1; change 'Beach' to 'Chiloe'.
Page 74; line 5; replace 'or U.' with 'ssp.'.; Line 12; replace 'few' with 'barely half'.
Page 75; 2 lines up, after 'tunic', insert '(brilliant white in Guernsey).
Page 76; Jellyfish. Delete the sentence referring to the Portuguese Man-of-war.
Page 77; Various Worms, line 1; replace 'at Clonque in Alderney' with 'in the four main islands'.
Page 109; para 2; delete 'and possibly also the Agile Frog'.
Page 113, para 3, line 6; delete 'Alderney and'.
Page 114; Wall Brown; line 3, substitute 'caterpillar' for 'butterfly'; Meadow Brown; substitute 'one extended' for 'two'; Small Heath; abundant, 'except in Guernsey'; Small Tortoiseshell; '4½cm'; Red Admiral, delete 'and Thistles'.
Page 115; Small Copper; after 'Two' insert 'or three'; last para; delete 'Berger's'.
Page 116; Moths, Emperor; delete 'Europe's largest moth,'.
Page 117; last para, line 4; substitute 'Also' for 'in Guernsey'.
Page 118; delete from 'line 1; Meadow' to line 3; 'larger'.
Page 120; The Centipede is now known as 'N. flavus'.
Page 122; para 1, line 3; delete 'a few'; para 2, line 2; insert 'Guernsey' as 1st. word; line 5 delete 'Little'; line 9; change 'breed' to 'bred'; line 10, delete 'Guernsey', and substitute 'until 1974' for 'and Herm'.
Page 123; para 1, for 'Little Auk' substitute 'Razorbill'; para 5, line 4; first word change 'black' to 'brown'.
Page 124; para 3, line 8; delete reference to Rookeries; para 4, line 4; substitute 'Hawfinch' for 'Linnet'.
Page 125; line 4; substitute 'spring' for 'winter'.
Page 127; change 'has' to 'had'.
Page 131; para 1, line 6; change 'The' to 'A' and add 'as yet unidentified' at the end of the papa.
Page 133, para 3, change '1974' to '1975'. para 4; change 'President' to 'Director'

# Addenda

Page 63, line 3; after 'lists' insert 'of mosses', line 4; after 'Crevichon' insert '(The list of Guernsey Liverworts was updated by Dr. Jean Paton in 1969).'
Page 65, para 2 line 2; after 'only' insert 'indigenous'.
Page 74; 9 lines up after 'islands' insert 'but which was finally lost in the 1987 hurricane'; 4 lines up; after 'today' insert 'in the wild'.
Page 75; 2 lines up, after 'tunic', insert '(brilliant white in Guernsey)'.
Page 115, Small Copper; after 'Two' insert 'or three'.
Page 117. Add 'in Guernsey' after the last word.

# A Natural History of Guernsey, Alderney, Sark & Herm

by
Brian & Dr. Jean Bonnard

© 1995
Brian & Dr. Jean Bonnard, BSc, DipEd, DIHom, HMD, FBIH, NMD, HMI(Retd).
The Twins, Le Petit Val,
Alderney, Channel Islands, GY9 3UU

Maps and photographs by Brian Bonnard © 1995

All rights reserved. No part of this publication may be reproduced, stored in a retrieval system, or transmitted in any form or by any means, electronic, mechanical, photocopying, recording or otherwise, without the prior permission of the authors

First published 1995

Published by
The Guernsey Press Co. Ltd, Guernsey, Channel Islands

ISBN 0902550-60-8

Other local books by Brian Bonnard;
Published by the author;
Flora of Alderney; a Checklist with Notes, 1988, with corrections; and additions to 1995. Price £3.50
Wrecked around Alderney, 1993. Price £3.95

Published by The Guernsey Press Co. Ltd.;
Channel Island Plant Lore, 1993. Price £4.95
Out and About in Alderney, 1995. Price £4.95

Published by Alan Sutton Ltd (a subsidiary of the Guernsey Press Co. Ltd.);
The Island of Dread in the Channel, 1991. Price £14.99
Alderney in Old Photographs, 1991. Now out of print
Alderney at War, 1993. Price £14.99
Alderney in Old Photographs; a Second series, 1993. Price £7.99

Front cover picture: Glanville Fritillary Butterfly
Back cover picture: Thrift and Prostrate Broom on cliffs

# CONTENTS

| | | |
|---|---|---|
| PREFACE | | i |
| INTRODUCTION | | v |
| CHAPTER 1. | The Formation of the Islands | 1 |
| 2. | A Brief Description of the Islands | 15 |
| 3. | The Settlement of the Islands | 29 |
| 4. | Wildlife of the Channel Islands | 53 |
| 5. | The Plants | 55 |
| 6. | Marine Animals | 75 |
| 7. | Freshwater Animals | 103 |
| 8. | Amphibians and Reptiles | 108 |
| 9. | Land Molluscs | 110 |
| 10. | Insects | 112 |
| 11. | Birds | 121 |
| 12. | Land Mammals | 127 |
| 13. | Ecology | 132 |
| 14. | Weather | 144 |
| BIBLIOGRAPHY | | 149 |
| INDEX | | 151 |

# GUERNSEY LILLY

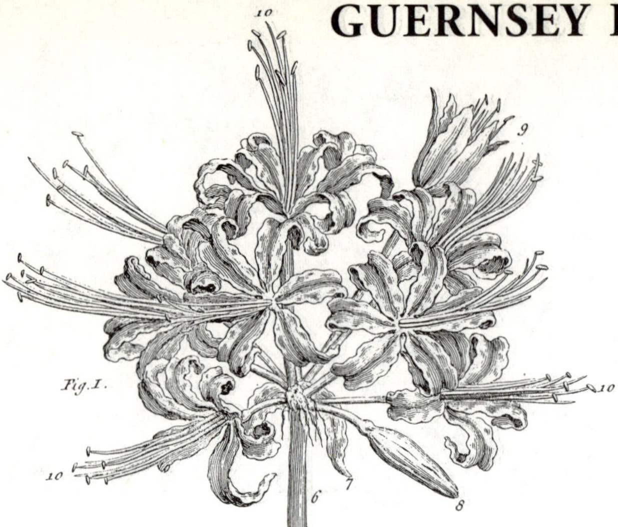

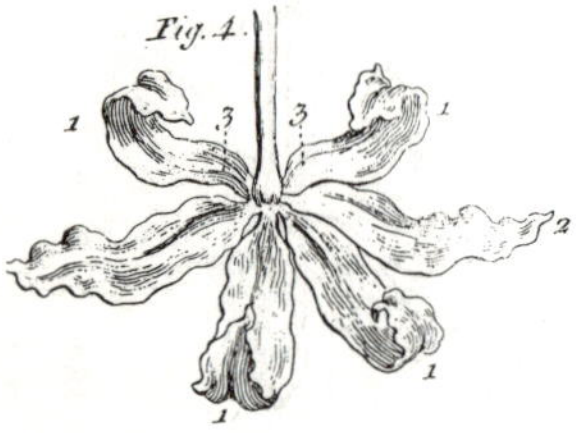

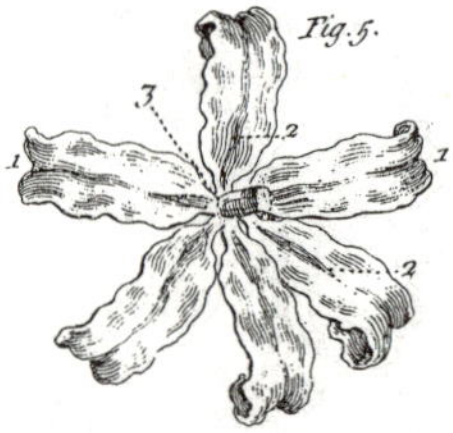

## FIGURE I.

IN this Figure the *Guernsay Lilly* is delineated in full Blossom, just as it was taken out of the Ground, intire in all its Parts, one Flower only being cut off.

1. Fibrillæ, *or small Strings of the Root.*
2. Fibræ *or* Radiculæ.
3. *The bulbous part of the Root.*
4. *The* Neck *or narrow part of the Root; both covered with the external* Involucra.
5. *The Leaves beginning to sprout on one side of the Stalk.*
6. *The* Caulis *or Flower-stem, which in this Figure appears more bent, than for the most part we observe it in the Plant its self.*
7. *The* Perianthium.
8. *A Flower not blown.*
9. *Another a little opened, to shew the Stamina and Apices just coming out.*
10. *All the other Flowers in full Blossom, with the Stamina and Apices drawn confused as they appeared to the Dessinateur.*
11. *The Root of the Petiolus of the Flower that was cut off.*

## Fig. IV.

HEre the Back-side of one Flower is exhibited; two of the *Petala* being drawn out at length to shew the Pinch.

1. *The* Extremities *of four of the* Petala *turned back, as they appear in this* View.
2. *The other two drawn out at length, to shew the undulation or pinching on the Edges near the Extremities.*
3. *The* Costa *or Rib running along the middle of the Flower Leaf.*

## Fig. V.

DEmonstrates the fore-side of a Flower in its full Bigness, the *Stamina* and *Stylus* being cut off.

1. *The* Petala *or Flower Leaves.*
2. *The* Sulcus *on the Inside.*
3. *The* Unguis *or narrow Neck arising from that Part called the* Umbilicus Floris.

By Dr. JAMES DOUGLAS, Honorary Fellow of the ROYAL COLLEGE of PHYSICIANS, LONDON; and Fellow of the ROYAL SOCIETY.

# PREFACE

The Bailiwick of Guernsey consists of the principal inhabited islands, Guernsey, (population in the 1991 census 58,867); Alderney, (population 2,297), Sark, (population c.600), and Herm, (population 113) and their several offshore islets, a few of which, Jethou, off Herm, Brechou, off Sark and Lihou, off Guernsey, are inhabited, each in the main by a single family and their dependants and staff. The uninhabited islets of Crevichon and Les Fauconnières off Jethou; "The Humps", off Herm; Burhou and Little Burhou, about a mile off Alderney; the Casquets about 7 miles off Alderney inhabited from 1724 to 1994 by the Lighthouse keepers; and many rock stacks and islets, inhabited only by seabirds and with a sparse flora and insect and invertebrate population, make up the remainder.

Each island and islet has its own unique flora and fauna often with a few species not found in the others. The differences are accounted for; firstly by the geological time at which they became separated from the continent of Europe and later from each other. Secondly by the restricted number of habitats present in each island or islet as their size decreases. Thirdly by the increasing effect of salt winds on the smaller islands; and lastly the effect that man has had on their ecology and environment over the millenia since the islands were first occupied.

Not surprisingly the number of different species of each class of plant and animal present diminishes as the size of the island or islet decreases.

Twenty-three centuries ago, Theophrastus of Eresus (370-286BC), a pupil of Plato and Aristotle, divided the natural world into three categories; Plants, Animals and Minerals. Nine volumes and part of a tenth of his writings, the oldest botanical works extant, have survived in the form of two 17th century Latin translations; *A History of Plants,* dealing with some 500 species, published in 1644 and *An Enquiry into Plants.* Despite the lack of a good lens or microscope, his observations were so detailed and accurate, that many of his conclusions are still accepted today. He is thus generally regarded as the "Father of Botany".

He said, for example, that; 'The phases of plants are so exceedingly diverse in nature and constitution that, to give a general definition of a plant, and that in a few words, is not possible', but drew the distinction that animals usually had an identifiable mouth and stomach.

Today plants, animals and minerals still form the basis of all the categories used. In a work such as this; more particularly so in the case of small islands; it is usual to include a review of the geological formation and early settlement of the places under discussion. This will be found in the present volume, followed by a section on each of the categories of wildlife, both plant and animal to be found here, with a general section on the varied habitats, ecology and meteorology of the Bailiwick.

The Romans introduced a number of herbs into the Channel Islands, for both culinary and medicinal purposes, as well as being the possible source of the ubiquitous rabbit. Later, in the 6-7th centuries the monks of the Cordeliers set up a number of religious houses in the islands where they would have cultivated their "simples" for the medicines they made. From Mediaeval times there developed a "Guernsey physic garden" of Nine Healing Herbs, planted in a 3x3 square with due ritual, which was cultivated in many cottage gardens, by both housewives and white witches, to provide medicines and materials to treat various ailments. Many of the ancient Norman-French names still used in the islands for fields, houses, etc. recall the cultivation or association with plants grown or found there.

There was a general belief throughout the islands that swearing at a plant or seed as it was planted enhanced its therapeutic powers. The nine healing herbs of the "Guernsey physic garden", found in most cottage gardens then, were; Hellebore, Lavender, Rosemary, Sage, Rue, Comfrey, Wormwood, Marjoram and Vervain and there is a mystic and magical significance to the 3 x 3 square format in which they were planted.

From Elizabethan times a manuscript *Book of Gardening and Medical Secrets*, has survived, written in 1589 by Thomas Andros of Les Annevilles in Guernsey, giving many 'receipts' for salves, tissanes and poultices with healing properties. This is described in some detail in *Channel Island Plant Lore* by Brian Bonnard, published in 1993. John Gerard's great *Herbal or a Historie of plants*, published in 1599 has an illustrated page on the *Garnesee Violets* (Sea Stock), a plant actually far more common in Alderney and the later 1633 edition has several references to plants found in Guernsey including Buck's-horn Plantain. A book in the Windsor Castle library, of flower paintings by Alexander Marshall, who died in 1682 records the Guernsey Lily and notes that the specimen was sent to him by General Lambert on August 29th 1659. There is what may be an even older drawing and description of the plant "The Golden Red-Lilly, called La Belle Guerneziese" engraved by Francis Hoffman.

Other records from Guernsey, mainly of plants made by apothecaries and other interested persons, go back to the early years of the 18th century, when a number of records and herbarium items were sent to famous naturalists in England and have survived in several collections. Amongst these are a book *Lillium sarniente or the Guernsay-Lilly* published in 1725 by Dr. James Douglas. There are a number of sheets of descriptions of Guernsey plants in the archives of the Linnean Society dated March 1782 and a Mr. Finlay sent specimens and descriptions to Sir Joseph Banks from Guernsey on 22nd February 1787. The herbarium of the Liverpool

Museum contains a sheet, originally from the herbarium of the Chelsea Physic Garden, from C.C. Babington of a specimen of one of Alderney's special plants, the Annual Rest-harrow, *Ononis reclinata*, collected there in 1828. Babington also records botanical visits to Guernsey by English naturalists in 1680-90.

Although a number of earlier records about Guernsey exist, very little in the way of investigation and recording of Alderney wildlife took place before the founding of the Guernsey Society of Natural Science and Local Research (now La Société Guernesiaise) in 1882 and most of what was written had only concerned the flora. Starting in 1889, a few years after its founding, the Society has published many articles in the annual *Transactions,* on various aspects of the natural history and geology of the islands, and a series of articles, from 1896 onwards, appeared about the flora.

The present volume makes no attempt to combine all of this published material; the reader should refer to the Bibliography for some of these references. Others are included in the text. Several booklets and reprints of important articles, are available from La Société Guernesiaise and in bookshops in Guernsey, including the Guernsey Airport shop.

Since the founding of the Alderney Society in 1966, a number of lists and booklets about the geology, birds, insects, other animal species and plants of Alderney, updated from time to time, have been produced and can be purchased from the Alderney Society Museum. Some are also available from the Alderney Airport shop, the "Bookshop" and the paper and souvenir shops.

La Société Serquiaise was founded in 1975, but became affiliated with La Société Guernesiaise in 1984, and thereafter has had a representative on its Council. The annual *Transactions* also carry a Sark section report.

Several small volumes about Sark's and Herm's natural history will be found in the shops in those islands.

To simplify matters for the majority of readers, the common names of both plants and animals have been used, (where such exist), with Latin names, (in italics), mainly for those which have no common name.

We hope that both residents and visitors will find this book of value in increasing their awareness and enjoyment of the many natural beauties of the several islands, and the many small islets and rock stacks, which make up The Bailiwick of Guernsey.

Jean and Brian Bonnard<br>
Alderney,<br>
November 1995

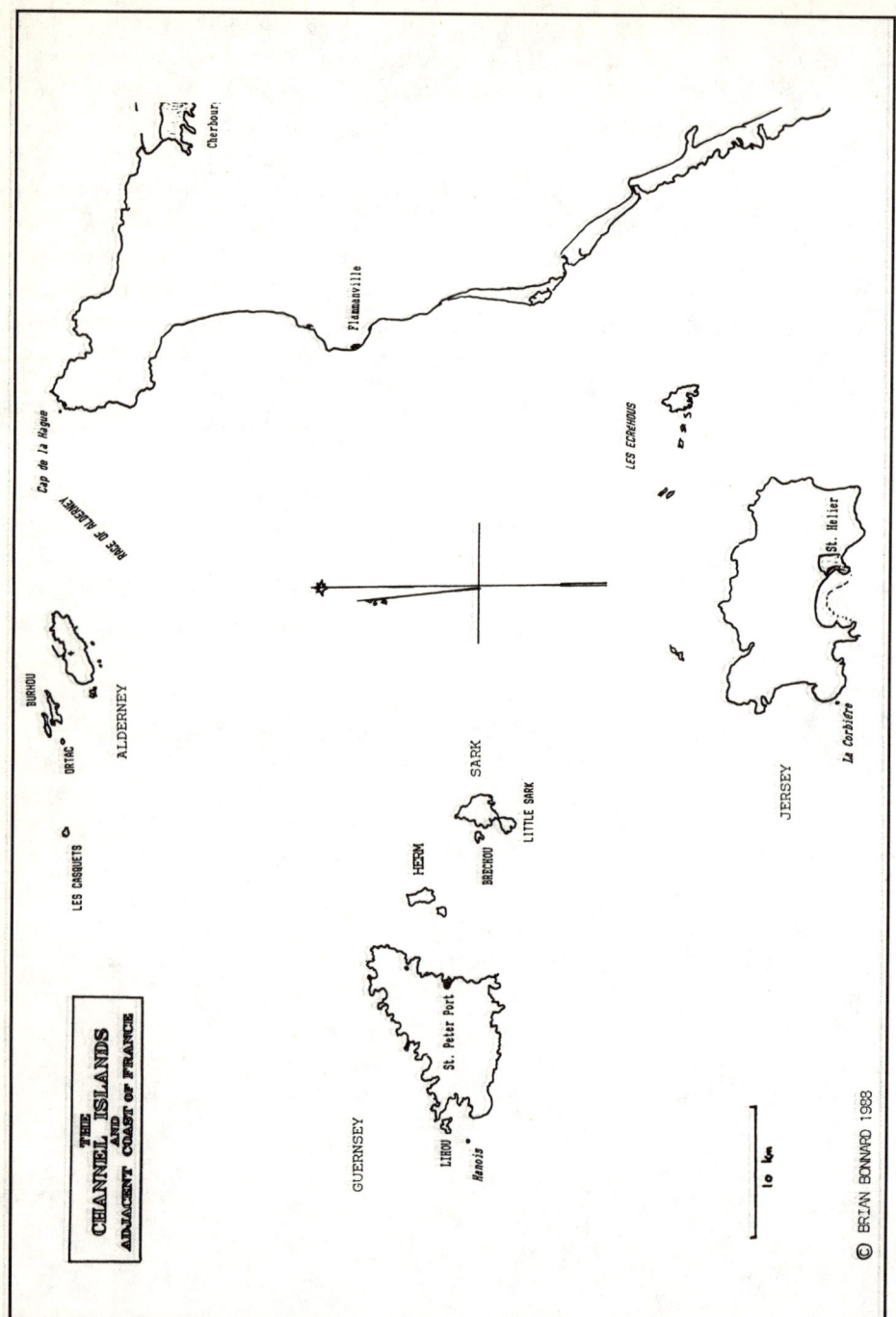

# INTRODUCTION

Descriptions of the physical appearance of Guernsey have appeared in the many histories and guide books to the islands; from Camden's *Brittania*, published in 1586, through Dicey's *An Historical Account of the Island of Guernsey, etc.,* (1751), Daniel Defoe's *Tour of the Whole of Great Britain, etc.,* (1762), Berry's *History of Guernsey* (1815), Jacob's *Annals of the British Anglo-Norman Isles* (1830), to the almost annual editions of *Black's Guide to Guernsey*, first published in 1866 and continuing until only a few years ago, with many other volumes both before and since.

In these a small section is usually devoted to Alderney, Sark and Herm, in many of the earlier works cribbed directly, even verbatim, from a still earlier volume, often written by a traveller passing on a ship bound for Guernsey or Jersey, who had not actually visited these islands. In these Alderney is frequently described as "Treeless", sometimes; "lacking in any important feature", "without rivers or streams", etc. etc., but it is rare to find any specific information about the natural history of the islands other than their coastal features, offshore reefs and rocks. Sark has been similarly recorded as lacking in trees.

In Guernsey Joshua Gosselin created an Herbarium and wrote an extensive flora of the island, inscribed in two notebooks around 1788. Fortunately both have survived, the first draft, (written from the back to the front in an old school maths notebook first used by him in 1755), being bought at an auction in Dublin in 1955 by Guernsey antiquarian bookseller, James Stevens-Cox. The Herbarium somehow came into the possession of Edgar Dupuy, a St. Peter Port pharmacist about 1900 and is now in the possession of La Société Guernesiaise who had received it in a parcel marked "A collection of dried plants, collector unknown", just after the last war, from a "Miss Marquand of King's Road". It lay in a cupboard untouched for about 25 years. The second, revised, notebook, a tiny leather bound volume 6in. x 3½ in. of about 180 pages, with the title page inscribed *Flora Sarniensis, or the Genera of Guernsey Plants, began in August 1788, by Joshua Gosselin,* was given to the Guille-Allès Library in 1919, with a similar MS book of his, *Conchologia Sarniensis*. Gosselin's list of plants was published by Berry in his History of Guernsey in 1815. This volume also contains the list of Guernsey "Shells", virtually all of which can be found in Alderney and the text of Dr. J. MacCulloch's 1811 paper in the Transactions of the Geological Society, on the Mineralogy of the islands of Guernsey, Alderney and Sark. The Flora was eventually transcribed by David McClintock and published by the Ray Society as

v

*Guernsey's Earliest Flora* in 1984, at the same time the parcel of dried plants was recognised for what it was and carefully investigated. It also contains a few Alderney specimens. It is now housed in a specially constructed cabinet and is the crowning glory of La Société's herbarium, which also holds Dupuy's own herbarium and a vast number of specimens from the whole Bailiwick, collected since it was formed.

The first detailed printed record of the Bailiwick flora is contained in C.C. Babington's *Primitiae Florae Sarnicae* published in 1839, which covers the three larger islands, plus Herm, Jethou and Crevichon, as well as Jersey.

In the mid 19th century, several members of the Lukis family in Guernsey excavated archaeological sites there and in Alderney. They also had some interest in natural history and F.C. Lukis, the father, supplied the list of 142 Guernsey lichens included in Babington's book and the lists of Guernsey fungi, fish, molluscs, beetles and butterflies, to Ansted and Latham for *The Channel Islands*, published in 1862. He also helped with the list of birds in that work. The family's archaeological records were written up by their father in 6 large MS volumes *Collectanea Antiqua,* now to be found at the Guernsey Museum and Art Gallery. The Alderney references appear in Volume 5 of these, and an old photographic copy of this part is held in the Alderney Society Museum.

Jonathan Duncan's *History of Guernsey,* published in 1841 has only some 22 pages devoted to natural history, in this large work. Most of this is concerned with the geology of the islands, but it also has a brief list of the birds and a much longer list of marine molluscs.

Ansted and Latham's book has a large section devoted to their natural history and contains detailed lists of most of the various classes of flora and fauna known at that time, with their distribution between the four larger islands, with Herm, Jethou and Crevichon records being lumped together as a fifth group.

The works of Ernest David Marquand over many years on a whole range of Bailiwick plants, animals and natural features have given us the best information we have from earlier times, indeed, in several spheres, his lists for Alderney species have never yet been repeated by later investigators.

Marquand, a Guernseyman born in 1848, eventually became a distinguished Naturalist. His family emigrated to New York in the 1850s, but after his father died returned to England, where he trained as a Solicitor and worked for a firm of London Solicitors. Office work proved uncongenial, not surprising for an already committed amateur naturalist.

In 1876 he gave up city life, and went to live at Brockenhurst in the New Forest, where he studied the flora and fauna of the area. Some of his work was included in Townsend's *Flora of Hampshire.* He left the New Forest in 1879, and went to Penzance in Cornwall. Here he continued his studies, entomology being his principal interest at this time. He soon became Secretary of the Penzance Natural History Society and at this time he gave many lectures, and contributed papers on entomology, conchology and botany to their *Transactions*.

After seven years in Cornwall he moved to Alphington in Devon. Sadly twelve months later his mother died, he and his brother then travelled widely in Germany, Austria and Switzerland, but after a year they returned to Guernsey in 1888, where he joined the Guernsey Society of Natural Science and Local Research, developed a great interest in the botany of the island and started a Botanical Section of the Society in 1892. He was elected its President from 1892-94.

In April 1896 Marquand married a Miss G. Boley of Ealing, at St. Martin's Church in Guernsey. He spent some of the early years of his marriage working at the Kew Herbarium and for the Linnean Society. Returning to the Channel Islands in 1899 he took up residence in Alderney for four years, but because of the need of a good education for his son, moved back to Guernsey until 1910, when he moved with his family to Paris. He worked for the Guille-Allès Library in Guernsey from 1903-6 identifying and re-arranging their Natural History Museum Collection.

His 500 page *Flora* published in 1901, was the result of seven years labour in the several islands of the Bailiwick, and, with his several updates published in *Transactions,* still remains the definitive work on the subject as far as Alderney is concerned.

His description of Alderney in 1901 as the least known of the Channel Islands to the outside world, makes interesting reading.

'It is customary to speak of it as a bleak and desolate spot, devoid of any single object of interest, and surrounded by an exceptionally tempestuous sea.'

He also referred to the fact that of the visitors to the Channel Islands less than five percent ever set foot in Alderney, and to many of the residents in the other Channel Islands, Alderney remains literally 'terra incognito'.

He felt that for city dwellers, and those brain workers seeking rest Alderney is in several respects without a rival, even in this favoured archipelago.

He described Alderney:-

'The coast scenery is extremely picturesque, and in many places hardly to be surpassed for wildness and beauty: the air is delightfully pure and bracing: there is plenty of sunshine and comparatively little rain: whilst above all there is an indescribable sense of liberty and freedom, which is altogether lacking in the other islands'.

'Owing to its situation at the entrance of the English Channel, Alderney has always been regarded as an outpost of great military importance, and enormous sums of money have been expended by our government in constructing a long chain of forts and batteries all round the low lying coast as well as in erecting a breakwater'.

'Westward from Alderney several groups of islets and rocks stretch out for many miles, and when viewed from the heights of Butes Hill, compose a picture of rare beauty. The uninhabited island of Burhou, is 'par excellence' the seabirds home.

'Further away, seven or eight miles from Alderney, glitters the white tower of the Casquets Lighthouse, marking the most perilous reef on the British Coast, where, as Shakespeare says of the Goodwins, ' the carcasses of many a tall ship lie buried'.

'The soil in some parts of the Island is deep and of excellent quality, but in others it is poor, and produces but thin crops. Except in the valleys that open out towards the north, there are few trees, and they do not attain any large size. Springs of excellent water abound, but streamlets are few in number and very small.'

Also according to Marquand:-

'Alderney possesses an exceedingly interesting flora, also that a visitor will find here in a single day's botanising a larger variety of really rare plants than in either of the other Channel Islands,

'Little if anything, was known about the wild plants of this out-of-the-way spot until the publication in 1839 of the first Flora of the Channel Islands, Professor C. Babington's little book, entitled *Primitiae Florae Sarnicae*. (Note; He was not aware at this time that Gosselin's Notebooks and herbarium had survived, although he must have read the list in Berry).

According to Marquand:-

'In every section of the flora Alderney differs from the U.K. and other Channel Islands, by the possession of plants peculiar to itself, and in many respects approximates more closely to the continental mainland, as would be expected from its geographical position.'

Many of the sightings recorded by Marquand in 1899-1903 are still valid today, for example, Nipplewort can be found at precisely the same location at Picaterre Farm as was recorded by Marquand during his time on the island, and the Rough Star Thistle, still occupies the same small site on Braye Common, not having spread in almost a century. By contrast, Stinking Onions, which he described as;

'"Rare' A patch about five yards square on the North-west side of Fort Tourgis. Also grows in grassy places in Victoria Street, at Government House, and in St. Anne's Churchyard. In these last situations, perhaps planted."

The plant, looking somewhat like a white Bluebell, its patois name Bllanche côneilles means just that, with its pretty white flower with a green stripe down the back of each petal, reached Guernsey about 1847. It was included in the Guernsey *Mauvaises Herbes Loi* in 1927 but removed in 1952. In Alderney it now occupies most hedges, roadside verges and banks across the island, and forms a carpet of white from March to June, even flowering as early as October or November and throughout the winter in some years. It is such a pest in gardens, spreading by bulbils as well as seeds, that it was included in Alderney's Mauvaises Herbes Law in 1952. It has now spread to the other islands and parts of the south coast of England.

Ernest David Marquand was most certainly a notable scientist, became a member of many learned societies, and received a number of awards. In 1901 he was elected an Associate of the Linnean Society of London.

G.C. Druce, (another eminent botanist who has also studied the Bailiwick flora) said of Marquand:- 'He tried to implant in others his love of nature.'

Marquand died in Devon and was buried at Totnes on February 20th 1918.

The generally mild, oceanic type of climate enjoyed by the Channel Islands now, and the fact that even during the Ice Ages, the glaciation did not extend this far south, have affected the range of plants and animals which can thrive in the restricted number of habitats and soil types.

There is no chalk anywhere in the islands, lime loving plants only existing in the areas of shell rich sand, thus comparatively few of the animal species which feed or breed on these plants, particularly insects and molluscs, are to be found here.

Alderney is the only island in the group with an appreciable amount of sandstone, extending across the North and East parts of the island and its Off-islands, from Raz, round to the north and west to Burhou and the Casquets the exposed rocks are almost entirely composed of this. There is also a very limited amount of peaty acid soils and there are few salt marshes, dune slacks, or bogs.

Freshwater bodies with the exception of Vale, Longis and Platte Saline ponds are man-made, mostly water filled quarries.

There are no significant rivers in any of the islands.

The natural tree population shows a scarcity of many woodland species which are common in Britain, and the calcicole, water and marsh plant flora is similarly reduced, as are the numbers of birds, insects and small mammals which favour these habitats.

In addition to the trees, there are about fifty flowering plants common on mainland Britain, which are not found wild in any of the islands, and about a dozen more which are very scarce. A much larger number of the plants less common in Britain also do not exist at all in the islands. Conversely there are about a dozen plants found in the islands which are totally absent from any natural habitat in the U.K., and a further forty-five or so, which are very rare in Britain, and then principally found only in the South and West.

Agriculture over the centuries has also been an important source of new plants, many imported inadvertently with seed. A majority of these adventives were annuals and, in recent years, better seed cleaning techniques and the use of herbicides has produced a sad decline in these species in U.K. Amongst the most noticeable is the decline of cornfield weeds, such as *Poppy, Corn Marigold* and *Corn Sow-thistle.*

Today these are more common in Alderney, where more traditional farming methods are still in use, albeit on a very limited scale now and where herbicides and pesticides are little used, than in the other larger islands or in Britain. Helped by this, five species of Broomrape, flourish there, now either rare or in great decline in the U.K.

Many of the rarer plants exist either as a small number of specimens scattered over a number of similar habitats, or in a very limited area perhaps in greater numbers. The existence of the microhabitats which occasion this makes a fascinating study as does the history of the spread of a species, or the failure to do so whilst thriving in a chosen spot.

With regard to the Fauna; the detachment of the islands from the mainland of Europe occurred in stages; with Guernsey, Herm and Sark forming one large island about 15,000 years ago, which later split up further as the water levels rose with the receding ice. As a result many mammals, gradually spreading northward and westward from warmer regions did not reach the area. Guernsey for instance has no moles, which are plentiful in Alderney and Jersey, whilst Alderney, Sark and Herm have no weasels. The stoat is recorded occasionally in Guernsey. None of the islands in the Bailiwick have foxes or badgers although foxes were hunted in Jersey until they became extinct about 1860, Hares became extinct in Guernsey about the end of last century. In fact the largest land mammal to be found in the wild is the rabbit, frequent in Guernsey, but common enough to be a pest in Herm and Alderney, with Alderney having a proportion of black rabbits in its population. These were also noted in Herm at the beginning of the century.

Hedgehogs were introduced into Guernsey probably in the 1850s and to Alderney about a century later. They have thrived and Alderney has its own unusual race of pale-spined animals in more or less equal numbers to the usual brown form. Black Rats were common in Alderney and Herm and were found in Sark to the exclusion of the Brown Rat in 1862, at which time they were very rare in Jersey, Guernsey and England. Today Alderney and Sark still have considerable numbers of this rodent, whilst Brown Rats are now common throughout the area. The field and wood mice, shrews and voles of the islands differ from those found in Jersey, France or Britain, having been isolated for many centuries. The house mouse however appears to be the same species.

Peat deposits occasionally uncovered beneath sandy beaches after violent storms and caves and megalithic tombs have yielded the bones of much larger beasts, from the ox and horse to deer and wild boar, as well as the remains of petrified forests.

Insects abound, helped by the generally low level of pesticide use. Numbers of these were probably imported over the centuries with agricultural produce and seeds. One butterfly, the Glanville Fritillary, is fairly common in the Channel Islands but confined to a small area of the Isle of Wight in Britain.

Unusual birds include two nesting colonies of Gannets, one colony only about 150 yards offshore from Alderney and the other about a mile out in the Swinge. Puffins, once present in their thousands, still breed on Burhou and the western cliffs of Alderney, and round Jethou, Herm and Sark. The Dartford Warbler, rare on the mainland, also breeds in the islands.

In the remaining chapters of this book, we will look at the formation, structure and colonisation of the islands. At their various habitats and the plants and animals which live in them and finally make a brief survey of the climatic conditions as far as our records exist over the last 150 years.

Gannets on Ortac

The Vale from the Air.

Herm & Jethou from the Air.

*Chapter 1*

# THE FORMATION OF THE ISLANDS

In the Quaternary Period, which started about 1-3 million years ago, the Channel Islands became separated from the European mainland several times during the various Ice Ages, as the sea levels rose and fell. Evidence of these inundations can still be seen in the exposures of raised beaches at about 30m, 18m and 8m, above present mean tide level, to be seen at many places in Guernsey, the 18m and 8m beaches are exposed at several places in Alderney and the 8m at the northern end of Burhou. There is also some evidence of the 8m beach on Herm and larger deposits at this level on Jethou.

The islands today form an archipelago in the Bay of St. Malo in three main groups. They are part of the Armorican Massif, the ancient hard rocks of Brittany and western Normandy.

Alderney is the principal island of the northern group, which form a chain extending from Les Casquets to Cap de la Hague, running more or less East-West for a distance of about 21 miles from the Cape. (Fig. 1).

The central group includes the remainder of the Bailiwick of Guernsey and the southern group, the Bailiwick of Jersey including the Ecrehous to the north and Les Minquiers to the south. The most southerly and easterly group of all, the Chausey Isles still belong to France.

If the present sea level were to fall by about 45-50m, the Channel Islands would all form an extension of France, extending to just beyond Les Casquets in the west and down to the Brest peninsula in the south, returning to the outlines shown in Figure 5. A fall of only about 30-35m would be needed to reunite Alderney and Jersey to France and the other Channel Islands to each other.

A number of authors have written on the geology of the Bailiwick, or at least that of Guernsey, since McCulloch in 1811. For many years Dr. G.H. Plymen's paper in the 1932 *Transactions* and his map was the definitive work. 1965 saw a new account by Dr. R.A. Roach who also contributed to the survey conducted between 1972 and 1980 by a number of geologists working on the British Geological Survey. The resulting map was published by the Ordnance Survey in 1986 at a scale of 1:25,000. The most up-to-date work, *An outline and Guide to the Geology of Guernsey* by Roach, Topley, Brown, Bland and D'Lemos, was published in 1991, whilst a booklet of more general appeal *Rocks and Scenery of Guernsey*, was published by La Société in 1993.

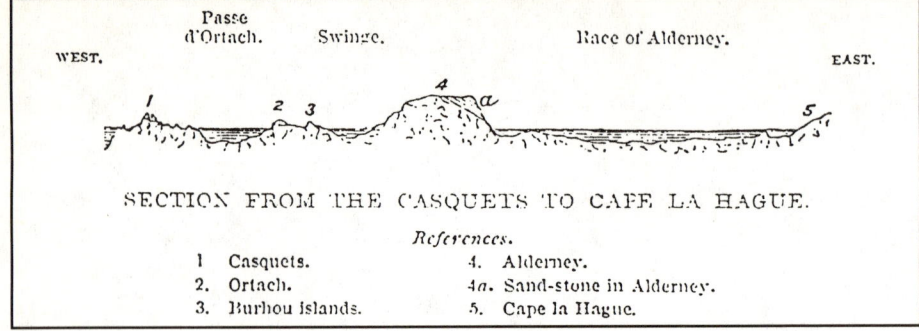

Figure 1. LES CASQUETS TO CAP de la HAGUE.

Whilst Jersey has cliffs on its northern side, and slopes gently towards the south, with only a small cliff area round the Noirmont headland in the south, Guernsey, Alderney and Herm all have cliffs on their southern sides, with the centre of each island a high plateau at about 95-100m, 85m and 65m respectively and slope down towards the north. Sark is a plateau rising to about 115m, surrounded on all sides by steep cliffs with only a few narrow valleys giving access to the interior.

The present situation of the islands, shown on the larger map at the beginning of this volume, may be compared with Figures 3-5, which show the approximate outline of the English Channel coasts at various periods since the last ice age ended.

This last interglacial period was from about 100,000 to 20,000 years ago and the rising waters from the end of that time gradually separated the Channel Islands and England from Europe. 80,000 years ago all the British islands were still part of the continent, occupying the space between two large river systems, one draining what are now northern France and southern England, with the Hurd Deep forming a large lake in this system, to the north of Alderney and the other draining southern Normandy and Brittany. (Fig. 2). As a result of this rise and of earth movements lifting the sea-bed, the Hurd Deep was still a lake about 10,000BC but the Atlantic shore had almost reached its western end. (Fig. 4). Much of the English Channel was formed by 8,500BC. Guernsey, Herm and Sark were still connected to each other but became separated from France about this time, whilst Alderney became an island (although much larger than today) and Guernsey/Herm and Sark were two separate islands by about 7,500BC. It seems unlikely that glaciation reached further south than the Bristol Channel, even in the Great Ice Age and there is no evidence of glacial rock formations in the islands.

Herm became finally separated from Guernsey about 4-5,000 years ago. None of the islands would have resembled their present day form at this time, being larger and mainly covered with deciduous forest. These differences in separation times help to account for the differences in the indigenous fauna and flora of the islands and to some extent, the presence and influence of man in the islands.

# OUTLINES OF THE ENGLISH CHANNEL

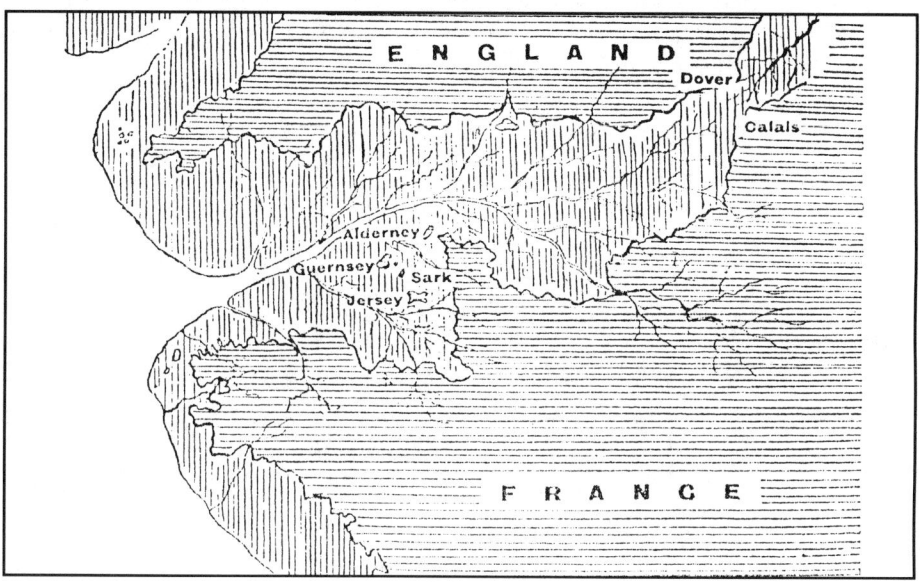

Figure 2. About 80,000 years ago
(After Geikie)

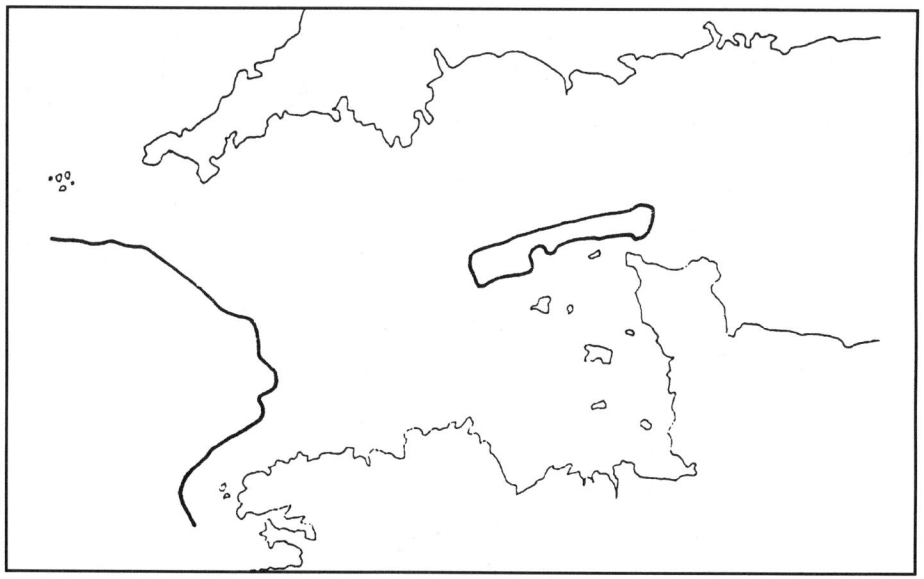

Figure 3. About 18,000 years ago
(After Renouf & Urry)

3

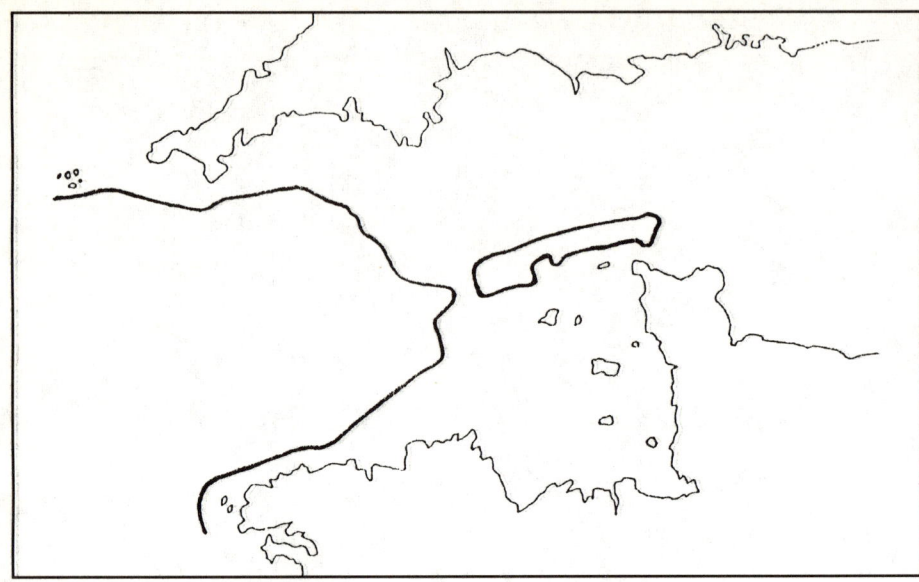

Figure 4. About 12,000 years ago
(After Renouf & Urry)

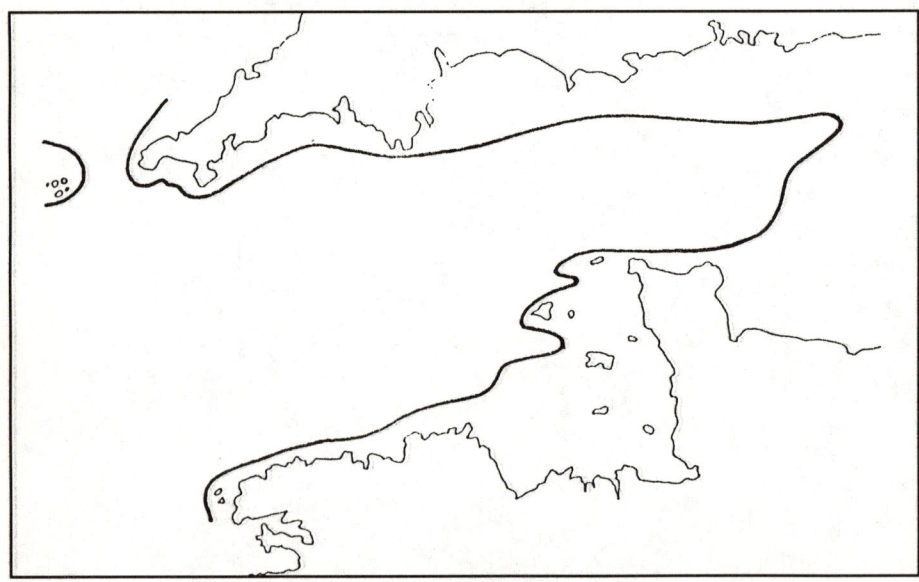

Figure 5. About 10,500 years ago
(After Renouf & Urry)

The Hurd Deep, about twenty miles north of Alderney, seems to be in the line of a river bed which would have drained the River Seine and many other tributaries from both sides of the Channel, into the Atlantic and is shown as a freshwater lake in Figure 3. There is a platform of harder rock extending about two miles out from the north coasts of Guernsey and Alderncy, parallel with this line and, with a depth of water over it of about 18m, is some 7 fathoms (13m) shallower than the sea bed a few hundred yards beyond to the north, showing the limits of estuarine scouring. It is now generally accepted that ocean beds have been rising at a measurable rate, due to the cooling, shrinking and folding of the earth's crust. The dykes erected in Holland in 1400, were under 1.5m of water by 1600 and the submergence of Roman roads along the coast of the Cotentin, shows that, mainly through a rise in the sea-bed, sea levels have risen by an average since then of about 45cm per century. Calculations for Jersey suggest a rise of about 30cm per century since 1300.

The flow of water sweeping in from the Atlantic and deflected up the coast of the Cotentin Peninsula, produces a tidal range of some 18m at St. Malo, which falls to about 13m in Jersey, 10m in Guernsey and 6m in Alderney by the time it reaches there some 1½ -2 hours later. This has helped to scour out the channels between Jersey and Normandy, Guernsey and Herm, Guernsey and Sark, Alderney and Burhou and between Alderney and the Cotentin peninsula. The swift currents and emergent, or barely submerged, rocks in these, account for much of the danger to shipping throughout the islands.

Rough weather in The Race. Cotentin Peninsula on the horizon.

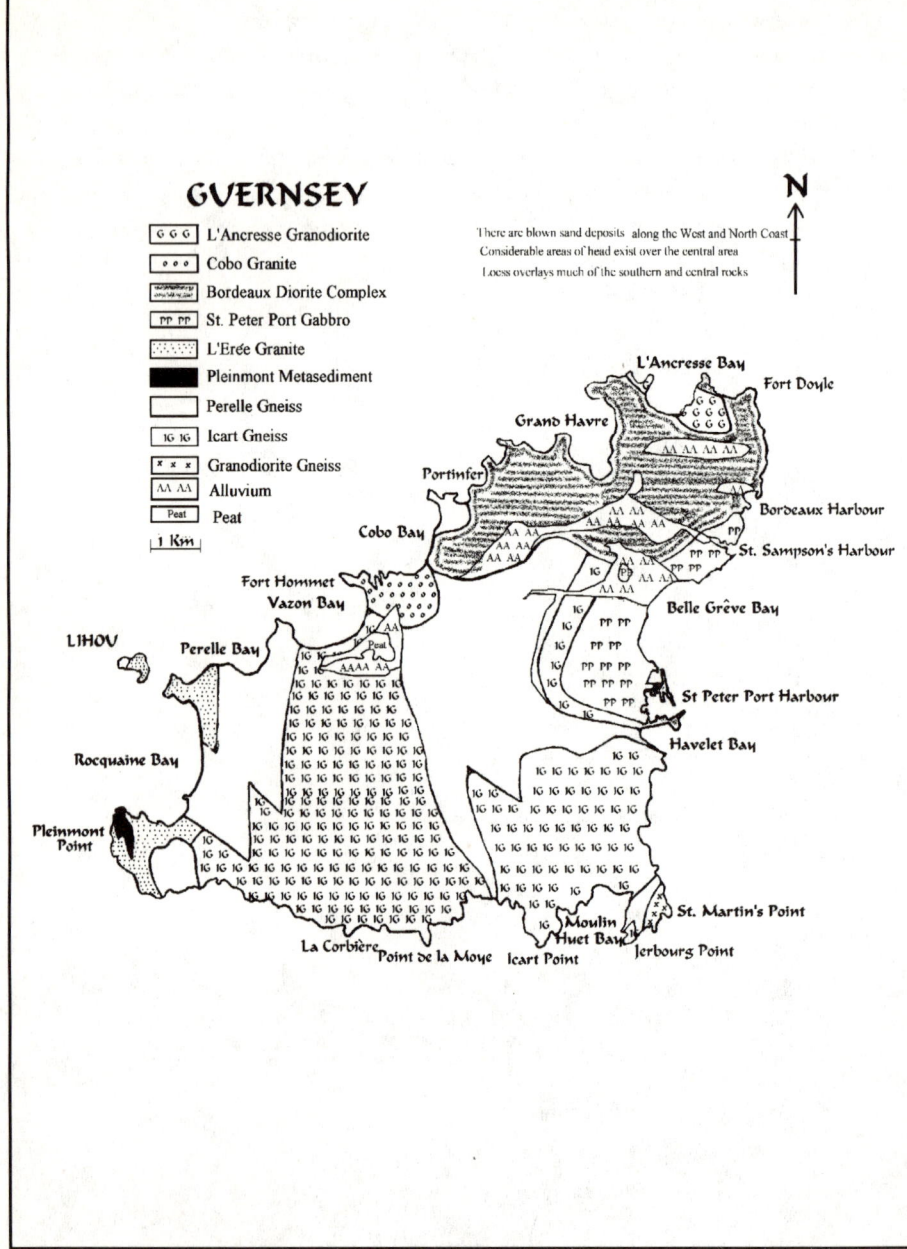

Figure 6. Geological map of Guernsey

# THE PRESENT STRUCTURE OF THE ISLANDS

*Guernsey.*

A high proportion of the southern and central part of the island is *granite augen-gneiss* of the Icart type, with a pink or pale grey colour. These are the oldest rocks in Guernsey with an age of about 2,000 million years. A band up much of the western coast from the L' Erée granite at Pleinmont, to Perelle and Cobo, where it is a coarse grained red granite, is about 550-650 million years old. At the south-eastern end of the island, the Jerbourg peninsula is mostly *granodiorite gneiss* of the Doyle type. Covering much of the parishes of St. Andrew, St. Peter-in-the-Wood and Câtel is another granodiorite gneiss the Perelle type.

A big part of the Vale and St. Sampson parishes are sitting on *diorite,* split almost in three by the *alluvium* stretching in a narrow band from Vingtaine de l'Epine to L'Islet and the Braye du Valle in the south and across the Clos du Valle further north. A third area of alluvium covers the area from Les Quartiers to the coast near the Château de Marais and also runs in a very narrow band from La Ramée to the Foulon cemetery. Part of the L'Ancresse area is blown sand overlaying a foliated fine-grained *granodiorite.*

There is a broad band of *gabbro,* a very dark igneous rock, extending from the south side of St. Sampson's harbour to Castle Cornet.

These are the principal blocks of underlying rock, but altogether about 45 types of rock, including about 15 more recent sedimentary types, make up the entire structure of the island. Around the coast, exposed particularly above the raised beaches are patches of *head,* formed by weathering of the gneiss and granodiorite.

Overlaying much of the southern plateau of the island is a layer of *loess* up to 5m thick.

Peat deposits are occasionally uncovered along the north western coasts after storms, especially at Vazon Bay. These contain the petrified remains of a forest.

Although Guernsey has little in the way of minerals with any commercial value and they have never been exploited, silver, copper, lead and graphite have been reported in the south-east, principally around Moulin Huet and Saint's Bay.

Much information about the geology of Guernsey has been published in the pages of *Transactions* over the last century or more. The reader is referred to these for further detail.

*Alderney.*

Ancient, crystalline, greenish-grey, *granodiorite,* whose age has been radiometrically dated to about 2,200 million years, makes up the western part of

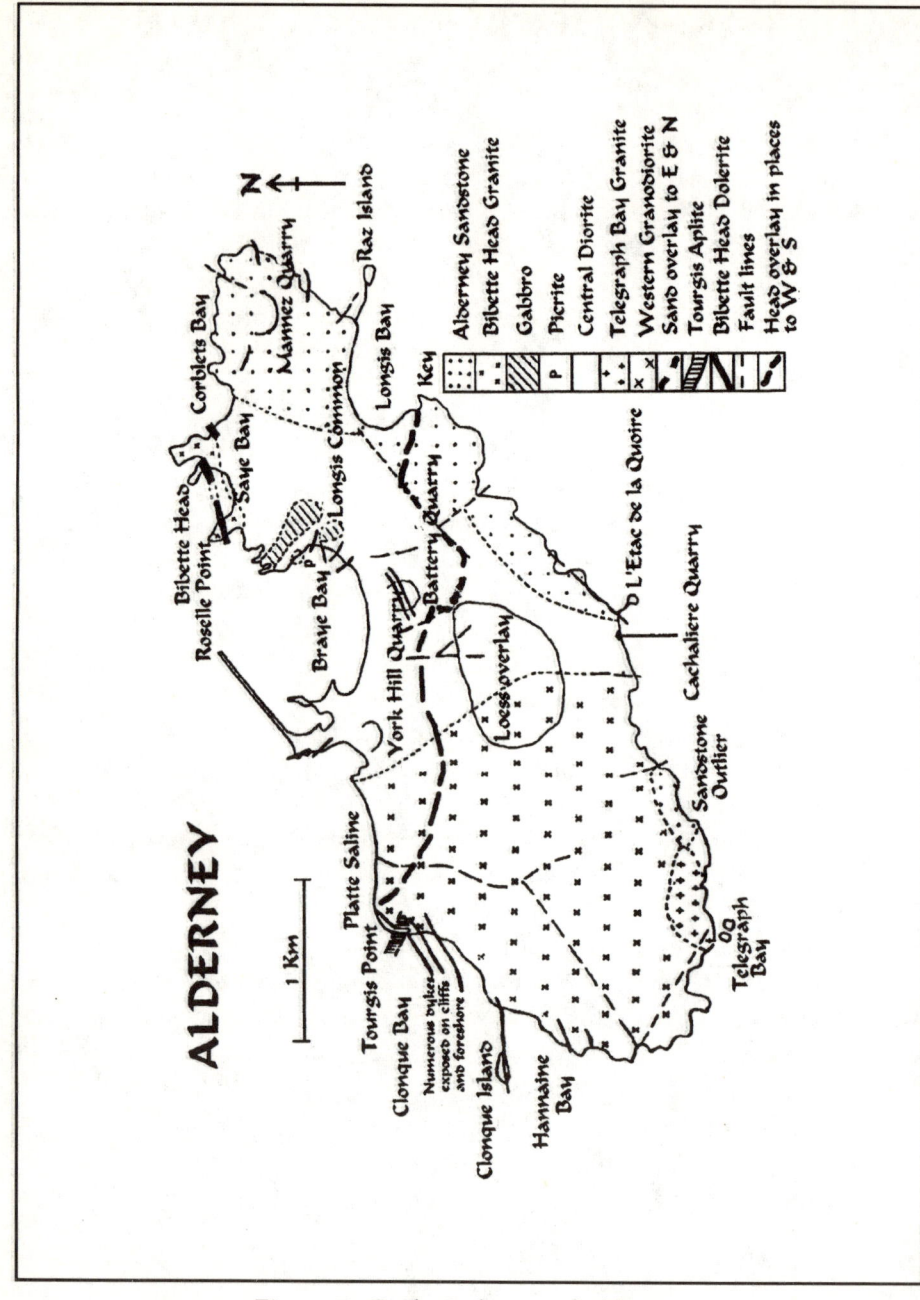

Figure 7. Geological map of Alderney

Alderney as a plateau about 85 metres high. Included within this are dark xenoliths, up to 1m across, of older rocks. Many thin seams of *aplite* may make up as much as one third of the rock, between Telegraph Bay and Hannaine Bay. Both rocks are cut across by dykes of pink, or light-coloured - ranging to purple - *porphyritic microgranite* containing crystals of *felspar* and *quartz*. The rock to the east of Telegraph Bay along to Cachalière is granite, also intruded by veins of aplite and porphyritic microgranite.

Faulted against the granodiorite and about 1,000 million years younger, the central complex is mainly composed of *diorite,* but also contains the *Bibette Head granite* and other, smaller masses of *gabbro*, with *picrite* and the unusual *orbicular diorite* at Roselle Point. Many parts of the southern and western cliffs of the island are overlain by patches of *head,* formed by weathering of the gneiss and granodiorite.

Much of the rest of the island is composed of *Alderney Sandstone*. This formation is generally unconformable, the coarser sediments resting on the older rocks, often with basal conglomerates. From Bluestone Bay to Cachalière the contact is partly upthrust upon them. In places it may be 400m thick. The main outcrop on Alderney extends around the east and south-east coast from Corblets Bay to L'Etac de la Quoir. There is an outlier to the west of this at Platte Côtil and from the Nannels through Burhou, Ortac and Les Casquettes to Les Noires Puttes, the reef is entirely of sandstone.

The sandstone is hard, generally of a light whitish to pink colour, the intrusions are principally of several types of *lamprophyte* and of *dolerite* and some of these are of the Carboniferous age. It is locally referred to quite inaccurately as 'Alderney granite'.

Ansted recorded in 1862, that "Alderney supplies almost inexhaustible stores of brick clay", but these seem to have been worked out before the end of the 19th century. He was presumably referring to loess deposits round the three, now derelict, brick kiln sites.

Longis and Braye Commons and the land from Saye Bay up to the north-west rim of Corblets Quarry are composed of a thick layer of windblown sand. Parts of Longis Common have a bed of *peat* at least 1m thick sandwiched between two layers of sand and the peat is normally exposed in Longis Bay, to the east of Raz causeway and occasionally at the Nunnery end of the beach near the German sea wall.

Platte Saline and the lower part of Le Petit Val, are probably beach sand and on Platte Saline this has been excavated as a sandpit, (now mostly backfilled), to a depth of about 10m. This contained much finer sand than the present beach, (which varies from fine grit up to 5-8cm pebbles), with many small mollusc shells. Below

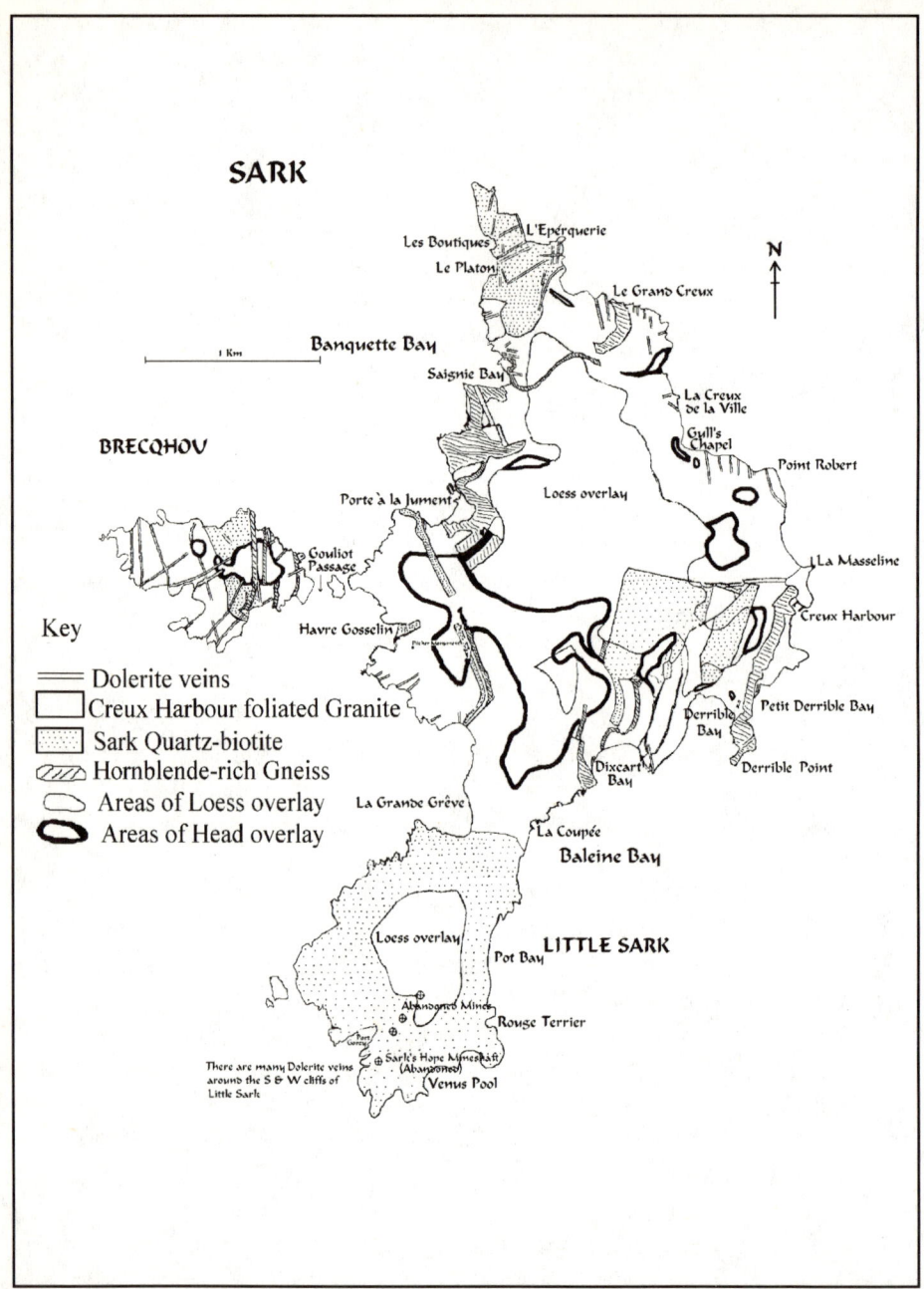

Figure 8. Geological map of Sark

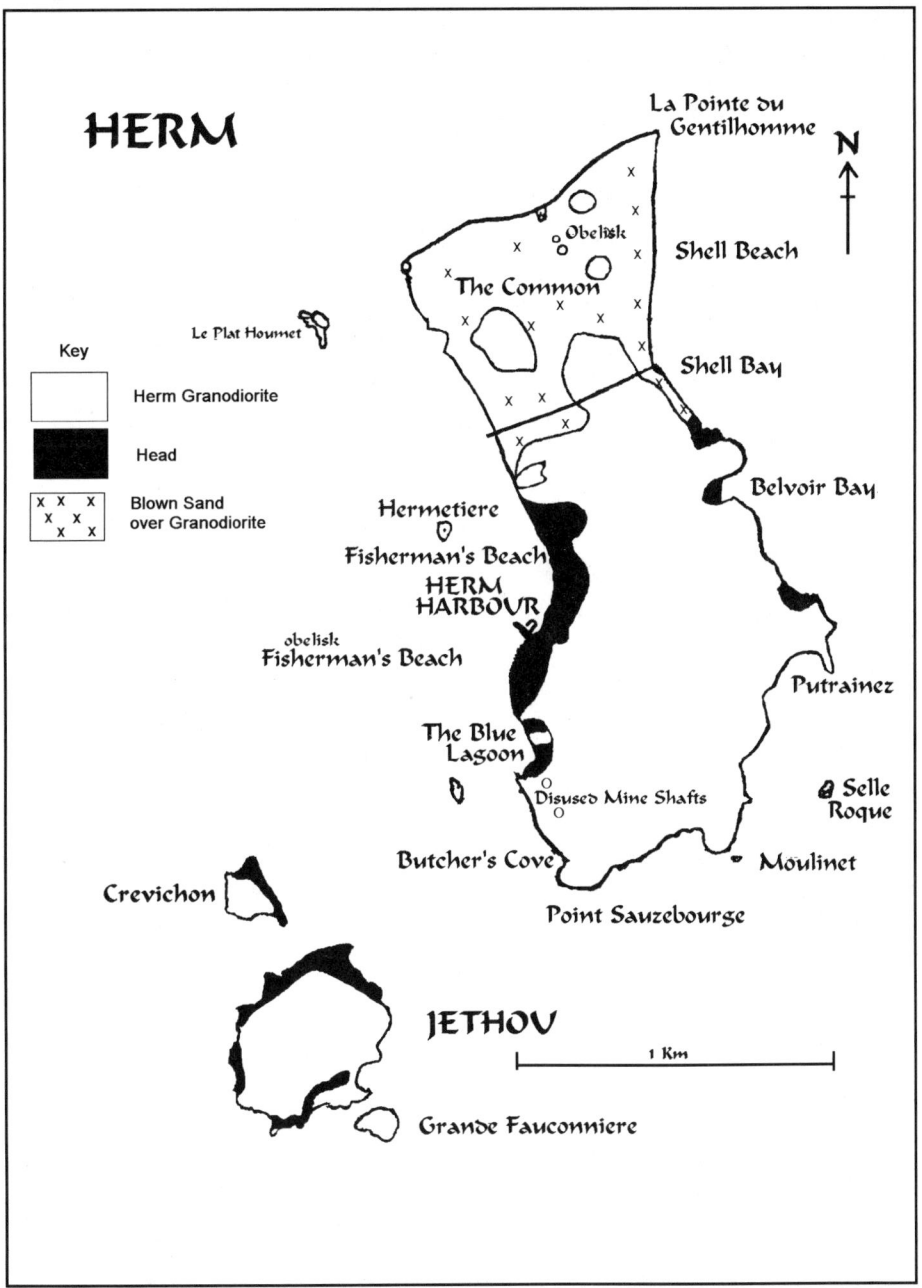

Figure 9. Geological map of Herm

this level are large sea-worn stones. The exposed walls inside the sandpit show evidence of many sand strata of varying thickness interspersed with beach pebbles.

A study of the soils types in the southern and western parts of the island, from 75 borings, was made by John Hazelden, MA of the Soil Survey and Land Research Centre, Silsoe, Bedfordshire, in April 1991.

He came to the conclusion that there were three principal soil types; (i). non-calcareous silty/fine sandy loess covering most of the plateau; (ii). windblown calcareous medium sand, covering most of the eastern end of the island and often overlying (i); (iii). *Head* of shattered rock, in some valleys and on hillsides.

He identified eight principal soil types, including one previously undescribed type. This he described as 'Longis' and identified it as 'calcareous stoneless sandy loam or loamy sand'.

There are no deposits of minerals with any economic value in Alderney.

## Sark.

Sark and Brecqhou are largely composed of a *quartz-biotite gneiss,* with small areas of hornblende rich gneiss, whilst Little Sark is almost entirely foliated *granodiorite.* All round the coasts there are intrusive dykes, mainly of *porphyritic microdiorite* and *felsite.* There are a number of caves round the base of the Sark cliffs including the famed Gouliot Caves with their treasure trove of Sea Anemones and other marine animals. (See the chapter on marine animals).

Like Guernsey the plateau is largely overlain by loess, here only about 2m thick, with a $p_H$ around 6 on the cliff tops and around 8 near the sea.

Silver and a small amount of lead were mined from a deep mine on Little Sark from 1835-1844. In Victorian times large nodules of Sarkstone, an amethyst like mineral which makes beautiful jewellery were found at Pot Bay. These are very rare now, but traces of pale mauve rock crystal can still be found in the cliffs there. Veins of copper and lead were found on Brechou in 1834, but were never mined.

## Herm, Jethou, Crevichon.

These islands and the many islets surrounding them, are almost entirely formed of an extremely hard coarse-grained *granodiorite,* with frequent dark xenoliths, the whole of the low lying northern third of Herm being overlain with blown sand, having the remarkable Shell Beach on its eastern shore. This feature will also be mentioned again in the chapter on marine animals.

Herm also has a history of mining (by the same company as Sark) from 1837, but a horizontal shaft some 140m long may possibly have been dug from the inside of a cave about 3m above HWM before 1833. By 1838 a 35m deep ventilation shaft had been sunk from the surface to reach this. The shaft was continued downwards for another 10m and a lode of silver-lead about 1m wide was found. Shortly after a deeper shaft further inland reached the horizontal one and was continued down for a further 35-40m with side shafts being cut in either direction and was yielding ore with a high copper content. All work ceased by the end of 1839.

Some clay suitable for pottery making exists around the top of one of the shafts. A small area on the western side and two smaller areas on the eastern side of Herm show weathered head.

## Stone Quarrying

Over the centuries stone quarrying has played a large part in the economy of each of the islands. In ancient times many Megalithic and Neolithic monuments were erected, particularly in Guernsey and burial chambers built in each of the main islands, often with some of the stone, especially the capstones, brought from more remote parts of those islands. Tools were fashioned from the harder smoother rocks in each island. Later, domestic building and subsequently, after the loss of continental Normandy by King John in 1204, throughout the period of fear of French invasion up to the early 19th century, the construction of watch houses, castles, fortifications, barracks, harbours, piers and sea walls in the principal islands, used vast quantities of local stone.

In Herm, from 1815, "Herm Granite" was quarried in considerable quantity. The stone proved to be harder than any English or Scottish granites and was used extensively in England for kerbstones and along the Thames Embankment walls. It was also used in the construction of the St. Peter Port Market Halls. By about 1840-50 some 400 men were employed on Herm quarrying by hand drilling and wedges. After about 1860, the development of larger, more efficient quarries in Guernsey gradually caused the demise of this industry.

Sandstone from Alderney has been found in the walls of the Roman Palace at Fishbourne in Sussex. Guernsey or Alderney "granite" can be found in many places in London, such as the steps of the Stock Exchange. During the Victorian era much stone was exported from these two islands, both as cut blocks for building and kerbstones and as crushed roadstone.

In Alderney from 1899, when the commercial quay was built, until 1940, this became the principal industry and major employer in the island, with almost half of the working male population being employed by the "Granite Company" when the island was evacuated in 1940.

Since 1945 there has been little quarrying in Alderney, except up to the late 1960s for maintenance of the Breakwater, whilst in Guernsey in the last few years, cutting of stone for the upkeep of the roads and maintenance of buildings, sea defences and harbours has been the principal work of the quarries. Local opposition to reopening old quarries has caused several of the recent major marina and land reclamation developments to be carried out with stone imported from France.

The deep holes left by quarrying over the centuries, scattered all over Guernsey and with four major ones in Alderney, form an important habitat for many aquatic plants and animals as well as, in many cases, a source of fresh water for the inhabitants.

Platte Saline Sandpit showing stratification.

*Chapter 2*

# A BRIEF DESCRIPTION OF THE ISLANDS

## 1. GUERNSEY

Guernsey is the second largest of the Channel Islands, the centre is situated at about 2° 35'W. longitude and 49° 27'N. latitude. It is roughly triangular in shape, with the north-west facing side the longest at about 9½ miles. The east side runs more or less north and south, is about 6 miles in length and contains both towns, the two principal harbours and the largest part of the population and industry, whilst the sparsely populated high cliffs of the south coast extend for about 7 miles. As already stated it has a high plateau area in the south and centre, occupying just about half of the land area and slopes down to the low sandy commons at the northern end. A large part of the western shore also bounds a flat coastal area which rises sharply to the plateau and has several salt marshes along its length.

In total area it is around 16,000 acres, or about 24 square miles, of which a little under ⅔rds is cultivated. Its highest point at Icart, where the oldest rocks are to be found, is about 114m (or 349ft).

The island was formerly two separate islands, Guernsey and the low lying island of Vale, joined by a bridge at St. Sampson's and, at low tide, across parts of the channel between them until, in 1803, under the orders of Sir John Doyle the arches of the bridge were filled in, an embankment built there and a causeway built at the western end to cut off the sea, as a defensive measure. The land thus reclaimed, the Braye du Valle was later sold by the government for £5,000 and gradually brought into cultivation. In this area the soil $pH$ is as high as 8.7 to 8.8.

The island is surrounded by dangerous rocks and reefs and is guarded at its SW point by the Hanois Lighthouse.

The capital of the island and the administrative capital of the Bailiwick, St. Peter Port, lies about halfway along the eastern side and is about 75 miles by sea from Weymouth, 25 from St. Helier in Jersey and 20 from Braye Harbour in Alderney. The nearest point of the French coast at Flammanville is about 30 miles to the east. Herm lies some 3 miles due east across the Little Russel channel, whilst Sark is to the south-east across the Great Russel, some 9 miles from St.Peter Port. All of the main islands are visible from St.Peter Port on a clear day. The island is divided into ten parishes, all of which, except St. Andrew, have a coastline.

St. Peter Port, usually called "The Town", has many steep rambling cobbled streets and long flights of steps between some parts of the town. To the south the land rises steeply from the harbour to the well wooded cliffs of Fermain, Moulin Huet, Saint's and Petit Bot bays. There is a fine undulating coastal path stretching all the way from the town to Pleinmont at the western end. Steep cliffs, tiny bays and a few old fishing harbours exist along this stretch which contains some spectacular scenery and an excellent selection of the island's fauna and flora. The main road runs well inland and the cliffs are reached by a series of narrow lanes, many running at right angles to the coastline. There are carparks with cafés and toilets close to the top of the cliffs at the end of some of these roads. A number are served to within a short distance by the local bus service. At intervals along this path there is evidence of watchtowers and fortifications, from mediaeval times, to the German concrete structures of the Second World War. The most prominent being the fire control tower on the headland at Pleinmont. The airport lies about 1½ miles inland, halfway along this side of the island, at an elevation of 104m.

Following the coast path round from the heights at Pleinmont one makes a steep descent to the area known as Land's End, the most westerly point of the Islands, near Fort Pezeries.

The broad sweep of Rocquaine Bay running east and north from here holds an ancient fishing harbour and a broad sweep of yellow sand with many rocky outcrops and tidal pools to delight all those, young or old who have an interest in the life on our seashores.

Part way along the bay is an offshore islet, topped by Fort Grey, a Napoleonic period fort one of the three true Martello Towers in the island, known locally as the 'Cup and Saucer', now a maritime museum and well worth a short visit. At the northern end of the bay another headland, L'Erée, is crowned by Fort Sausmarez with another German fire control tower built on top of the old 'Martello' tower. A few yards from the road just before this, the visitor would do well to pay a visit to the Neolithic burial chamber known as the Creux des Fées. On the point itself is a car park with a memorial to seamen lost in the wreck of the *Prosperity* in the narrow ½ mile channel between here and Lihou Island just offshore. At high water of spring tides there is about 10m of water in this channel and it dries out for as much as four hours between tides, allowing visitors access to the island along the causeway. At neap tides the depth may only be about 3m at high tide but the causeway does not clear for 3-7 days. Either side of the causeway look for the beds of Eel-grass or *Zostera*.

Geologically the rock of the island is a little older than most of this part of Guernsey. The remains of a 12th century priory dedicated to Notre Dame, (the Virgin Mary) are on the island, together with a modern house. Lihou is about 40 acres in extent and for many years was home to a flock of seaweed eating North Ronaldshay sheep, numbering about 80 by 1984. They were removed to Guernsey then and the pasture, brambles and other wild flowers have greatly benefited from their removal. The increased amount of scrub growth has also increased the number of birds found on the island. The sheep may often be seen on the old airfield site at L'Erée, only a few hundred yards away.

Continuing in a north-westerly direction, L'Erée Bay is backed by the Shingle Bank, home to a number of less common plant and animal species. These will also be dealt with later A short distance inland from the northern end of the shingle bank is the old Fish Factory, with a saltmarsh just behind it and a few hundred yards to the north again the larger extent of the Clare Mare with its wonderful meadows of Loose-flowered and other orchids, Common Adder's-tongue ferns and other marsh plants. La Société have established a nature reserve here with a hide, to allow the numerous bird species which nest there to be viewed without disturbance. A little further inland, up the road behind the old Fish Factory, the Silbe Nature Reserve is also worth a visit. Next comes Perelle Bay a small sandy bay with many rockpools at low tide. Fort Richmond and the derelict Fort Le Crocq are on the next headland. The broad sandy curve of Vazon Bay has its buried peat beds and the stumps of ancient forest trees exposed every few years after freak storms. The marshy area of La Grande Mare lies on the other side of the road round a considerable length of the bay. Part has been drained and the large complex of the Vazon Bay Hotel and golf club built in the last few years. The bay has Fort Hommet headland at its northern end. In the short turf on this headland the careful searcher will find a number of rare plants, including Guernsey's two special miniature ferns, the Small Adder's-tongue, *Ophioglossum azoricum*, and the even smaller Least Adder's-tongue, *O. lusitannicum*, which is found only in Guernsey and the Scilly Isles.

There are many acres of glasshouses in this part of the island, still known as Vineries and in earlier times growing grapes and then, for at least 75 years until recently, huge crops of tomatoes, most being exported to England. Much of this trade has now been lost to Dutch produce and the principal crop now is flowers for the English markets.

Next comes the tiny Albecq Bay with the Trepied Dolmen on the small hillock behind it and then the broad sweep of Cobo Bay with many rocky outcrops offshore, a wide sandy beach close to the road and a vast number of rock pools to explore. On the top of the hill on your right you will note an old watch-tower, Le Guet, surrounded with pines above a large disused quarry, from which the beautiful red Cobo granite which extends all the way up the coast to Port Soif was extracted for building most of the older local houses. There are some spectacular sunsets to be seen from Cobo, with the red rock of the outcrops in the bay glowing in the evening light. The several small bays from here to Grand Havre, the point where Guernsey and Vale Island are joined, are mostly almost circular, sandy and backed by dunes. Swimming here is safe and usually uncrowded. At the causeway just before Vale Church, a large saltmarsh is on your right, the Vale pond, with another hide at the roadside provided by La Société for the convenience of bird watchers. Most of this part of the Vale Parish is taken up by the flat sandy area of L'Ancresse Common, home to the island's main golf course, many Martello towers, several quarries, small fishing harbours and a number of Neolithic Dolmens. There are many small water-filled former quarries in the underlying hard rock of the Vale parish.

You reach the northern extremity of Guernsey at Fort Le Marchant and turning south soon come to the commercial and industrial area of St. Sampson with its shops, harbour, ship-yard and fuel oil and liquid gas storage areas. Beyond this the broad rocky sweep of Belle Gréve Bay with a huge area of rocks and pools exposed at low tide, brings you back to St. Peter Port with its marinas and harbour.

Inland, Guernsey has a number of wooded and well-watered valleys, the principal ones being Talbot Valley with its old water mills and Fauxquets Valley both in the parish of St. Andrew. Whilst in this area be sure to visit the Ron Short Trail in the National Trust Reserve in the Talbot Valley.

The island's main reservoir, with an interesting assortment of wildlife, occupies much of the parish of St. Saviour. These and the southern parishes are the principal pasture lands for the herds of Guernsey cattle. Here the soil is generally slightly acid to neutral, with a $p_H$ varying from about 6.4 to 7.4. They also have many Vineries, but not generally in such great concentration as the northern part of the island. The north-sloping land from the upper parishes down towards the north is generally more acid with $p_H$ varying from 5.4 to 6.4. The lower northern part of Guernsey has many small streams known as *doüits* running across it, frequently in channels alongside the roads, several marshy areas and, as noted above, many small water-filled quarries. Here the soil is mostly alkaline with a $p_H$ up to 8.8 and calcium levels around 10,000+ ppm on the sandy commons. In this area too there are small bands of 'black sand', generally running E-W, where the $p_H$ is similar but calcium levels are only around 1,200 to 1,300 ppm.

## 2. ALDERNEY

Alderney is a more or less rectangular island, pinched above the middle, just over 3½ miles long by just under 1½ miles wide at its widest. Lying with its long axis running NE - SW and the centre roughly at 2° 12'W and 49° 43'N. In area it is just under 2,000 acres. The island lies about 60 miles due south of Portland Bill and about 8 miles due west of Le Cap de la Hague, in the entrance to the

English Channel. Due to its proximity to more open, deeper, water than the other islands, it has a smaller tidal range. The waters of the Atlantic, sweeping into the Bay of St. Malo from the south-west encounter shoal water and narrow channels and are turned and reflected by the Normandy coast. As already noted, this gives a peak spring tidal range of approximately 18m at Mont St. Michel which gradually falls off, being only 6m by the time it reaches Alderney about 1½ hours later.

To the south of this axis the land is a plateau at roughly 80-90m with steep cliffs along the west and south facing coasts, indented by many small bays, most of which are almost inaccessible from the land. The projecting headlands drop almost vertically to the sea and it is not possible to walk around the base of many of them even at extreme low water. There are also a number of steep valleys each carrying a tiny stream. On the north side of the axis, the land slopes down quite steeply to the north and is intersected by six wooded valleys which each have a small stream running down them and two dry valleys descending from Les Rochers and the golf course, to Braye Bay.

The whole island is tilted slightly geologically, dipping towards the NW, it is surrounded by dangerous reefs and offshore rocks. 6-8 knot currents run through the narrow channels of The Swinge, properly known as Le Passage au Singe, which separates it from the rocky reef stretching from the Nannels to Ortac and the Casquets. It includes the offshore islands of Burhou and Little Burhou about a mile away from Alderney. The Race, again, properly known as Le Raz Blanchard, which separates the island from France and is about 6-7 miles wide at its narrowest point. There are further narrow, comparatively shallow and equally dangerous channels between Burhou and Ortac and Ortac and the Casquets. This last lies in the main shipping route between England and Guernsey and points further south into the Atlantic Ocean.

To complete the physical details in outline, starting at the north-west corner of the island below the huge bulk of Fort Tourgis and travelling round clockwise, we come immediately to the remains of a pond on Platte Saline, at the outfall of the principal stream of the island. This originates at L'Essoure, just below the plateau near the airport (elevation 87m, 266ft.) and passes almost immediately into Rose Farm valley, (Rose Farm, was probably the first enclosed farm to be made on the island), which further down becomes Le Val de la Bonne Terre. The name is a misnomer, it is truly "Terre bonne pour rien" good for nothing land, in this part. This is steep sided, bracken infested and quite heavily wooded. Here there is a mill leat, now become a marsh, which held the power source for the Watermill below. A mill has existed on this site since at least the 12th century and the remains of the last, (1760) mill can still be seen about 150 yards from the shore. In recent years the need for water for human consumption in the island has resulted in much of the flow of this stream being pumped to the reservoir and storage tanks and as a consequence Platte Saline pond, for many years from the 1960s, gradually turned into an overgrown, scarcely even marshy area, only a few yards from the beach, the waters draining away through the sand. Extremely wet autumns/winters in 1993 and 1994 went a great way to restoring the pond and surface water remained for most of the summer, sufficient for a *Mallard* to hatch nine and rear seven young in 1994. Plans are proposed to restore the pond by removing much of the accumulated silt and vegetation, during 1995 or 1996. In 1995 the wettest January for 10 years and total rainfall at 160% of the twenty-year average for the first three months of the year, added to the already large area of open water and, at least at the time of writing, in May, has restored the pond to its former size, some 60-70m across. Two pairs of Mallard reared families here in 1995 and Teal and other birds were seen on the water on several occasions.

The area gets its name from the fact that there were salt pans here at an early period and the area was also used as an *épérquerie* or salting and drying area, for mackerel and conger, some of which were exported to England. A tax was paid to the crown for this use from at least the 14th century.

The second valley, Le Petit Val, is in two parts. The first part carries a road and zig-zags down from the Town to Platte Saline. The lower half of the western part carries a very small stream, (originating in a spring on the hillside above), in a stone gully at the side of the road, which once joined the mill stream just below the junction of this road with Platte Saline and, when the Watermill was in use, was turned along the base of the steepest slope in an artificial *doüit*, the line of which can still be traced, to add its volume to the mill leat. The more eastern part originates at the edge of the town, runs under the road in one of its bends, at which point it feeds a large cattle drinking trough in a dip known as *Ladysmith* and then supplies a stone lined public wash place, known as a *lavoiret*, now flowing down through a steep, wooded valley to discharge in some volume into the middle of Platte Saline in another marshy area where, after supplying a newly made ornamental pond, it sinks into the sand and at low tide can be seen trickling out through the shingle along quite a wide area of the beach. The water from below the lavoiret was also seemingly carried across to the mill stream in the same artificial doüit at one time.

The third valley also carries roads, for parts of its length, runs parallel to these two and originates from a spring, formerly in Little Street. The stream now runs in a conduit under Little Street (formerly Rue des Vaches), under Marais Square, a former marsh as the name implies, under Connaught Square (formerly St. Anne's Square or Royal Square) and beneath the Island Hall, originally the Governor's residence and whose basement it still floods from time to time. It continues again from the Valley Gardens below the Church and then in a gully at the side of the road in Le Vallée [1], later returning to a stream-bed in a very steep sided wooded valley, Le Val Vert Courtil, whence it reaches Platte Saline towards the eastern end and discharges through a conduit, under the German sea wall, onto the beach.

The largest of these parallel valleys, Le Val, runs from the top of the High Street down to the sea at the harbour. The road runs along the western slope of the valley, well above its bottom, which bears no obvious stream now, the water course being in a closed culvert. An open Victorian brick conduit can be seen here in some old photographs. Originating at the same point from the High Street, Le Val Reuters runs off towards the east and soon curves down through a heavily wooded valley running back in a north-westerly direction.

This carries a small stream fed by several springs en route and becomes a deep valley known as La Fontaine David, the two valleys being collectively known as The Water Lanes, water from which discharges onto the beach in Braye Bay, near the western end.

A further watered valley is Valongis, the spring originating in a quarry in the upper part and supplying a cattle trough and possible lavoiret lower down.

This stream then runs in a culvert, under the Banquage housing estate and discharges in the middle of the curve of Braye Bay. The remaining two, dry, valleys run down the blown sand area from the top of Les Rochers and the golf course, to the eastern end of Braye Bay. The town of St. Anne occupies most of the north facing slope between Le Petit Val and Val Reuters.

The middle part of the coastline in this area just described is dominated by the huge 800m long wall, the remaining half of the Victorian Breakwater, partly enclosing Braye Bay, the eastern end of which is completely overshadowed by the largest of the Victorian forts, Fort Albert, atop Mont Touraille. From the Fort the whole eastern part of the island is also overlooked and is seen to consist of several rocky headlands separated by small bays and two large, curved, sandy bays.

At the far end is the Lighthouse, built in 1912 overlooking the site of Alderney's most famous wreck, the four-master *Liverpool*, which sailed straight onto Les Hommeaux Florains in 1902. This eastern end of the island has shallow soil overlying the sandstone, the stratifications in which give great interest to the rocks, both on and offshore and which also form a number of offshore islands and dangerous reefs. Inland, there has been extensive quarrying in the past, leaving a number of fresh-water filled areas, removing all trace of some former shallow valleys.

Turning south-west, there is a narrow coastal strip only a few feet above the shallow rocky beach with a few tiny sandy areas showing at low tide, extending

1 (Named after the Le Vallée family and not a misuse of gender)

for about ¾ miles to the great sandy sweep of Longis Bay. Protected on the east by the Isle de Raz with its Victorian Fort and causeway and, on the west, by the great bulk of Essex Hill, topped by Castle and Fort, which forms the eastern end of the plateau.

Longis was the only harbour in the island until work was started at Braye in 1734 and had been in use since Roman times or earlier. The remains of the stone jetty, which was rebuilt in 1661, can still be seen at low tides. The bay is now backed for most of its curve by the German anti-tank wall which separates the beach from the sand dunes whose character it has considerably affected. A stream was shown on old maps, originating above the Longis Pond and draining from it into the centre of the bay. Fresh water still oozes up from the sand here at low tide, but all trace of the stream bed has vanished from the common behind the wall.

Continuing SW for another two miles is a series of about a dozen small bays below high cliffs, whose beaches, of various types of pebbles or sand, differ considerably. These are all very difficult of access from the cliffs and are best appreciated from the sea. At intervals along this coastline are four short, steep valleys, each with its small stream. At the southernmost tip of the island, two large offshore rocks, Fourquie and La Nache shelter three sandy bays, the western one, Telegraph Bay is accessible from above, thanks to the provision of steps, cut into, or formed on, the cliff face about 1900, so that use can be made of this fine sheltered, south-facing beach and today maintained, from time to time, by the efforts of the Junior Militia and occasional visiting army units. At the present moment the lower end has again been washed away and the access to the beach is somewhat hazardous.

Turning now NW and still above towering cliffs, we come to the largest of the southern valleys, La Vallée des Trois Vaux the straight, main arm of which has a gentle slope downwards to the top of a small cliff overlooking its tiny bay, but precipitous sides rising to almost 100m. Opposite the exit of this valley are the offshore rocks Les Gardiens, or The Garden Rocks, otherwise known as Les Étacs, with their Gannet colony much in evidence from the end of January to October. Finally we turn due north through The Swinge, below the precipitous cliffs of Le Giffoine, a plateau which overlooks Hannaine Bay and the islet of Clonque and finishes in a dry valley and then NE along Clonque Bay passing the last of the streams, that of Le Vau Pommier, running onto the beach through a beautifully constructed, brick, Victorian tunnel, known as the Blue Bridge, under the track leading to Fort Clonque and emerging at the bottom of one of the old cobbled causeways used to bring vraic up from the beach in former times. At low tides, the curve of Clonque Bay, from the island bearing the Fort to the projecting low reefs below Fort Tourgis, becomes a vast area of shallow rock pools and sandstone ridges intersected with many dykes. It is possible to walk along the shingle beach from some 150 yards south of the Clonque causeway, all the way back to Platte Saline at all states of the tide and en route one can see evidence of both the 8m and 18m raised beaches in several places along the cliffs.

The most fertile areas of Alderney are principally on the plateau, in two areas known as La Grande Blaye, along the south coast and La Petite Blaye, along the west coast. In earlier times this area was farmed individually on an open field system and an area of about 500 acres was devoted to this. Most of the soil on the Blayes is slightly acid, $p_H$ about 6.5, with a few small areas amongst the heathland where the $p_H$ is more than 7.5-8 and others where it is just about neutral. The remaining land was held communally and used for grazing, gathering turf, furze (gorse) and fern (bracken) for bedding. Today the Alderney Airport occupies 140 acres of this prime land and agriculture has also sadly declined, assisted by the change in feeding habits brought about by the availability of tinned and frozen food and rapid, refrigerated, transport of meat, fruit, dairy products, etc. Most vegetables can now be imported more cheaply than they can be grown and with greater predictability of supplies.

The only areas in the island where the soil is alkaline are the sandy commons, dune areas and along parts of the east coast, where the crushed shells of many small molluscs bring the $p_H$ to about 8. Even along the east coast some areas are acidic, their area is easily noted by the presence of the pink/red leaved, white flowered English Stonecrop, as opposed to the green leaved, yellow flowered, Biting Stonecrop or Wall Pepper and also small patches of Heather and Ling.

## 3. SARK

Sark is approximately 3 miles by 1½ miles and has an area of 1,274 acres. It lies at 2° 22'W, 49° 26'N. It is a self-governing feudal fief, held directly from the Crown, by an hereditary Seigneur. It is basically a wave-cut platform almost entirely surrounded by precipitous cliffs with only a few places where landing is practicable. There are many caves at their foot, some, such as Victor Hugo's Cave on the west coast, only accessible by sea. The earliest landing place was near the NE tip of the island at L'Epérquerie. The Creux Harbour, on Sark's eastern coast, was built in the reign of Elizabeth I and is one of the smallest harbours in the world. From the landward side it can only be approached through a tunnel cut in the rock at the bottom of the steep half-mile ascent to the plateau and the village centre. Just before the last war a new landing place was started nearby, in a small bay on the other side of the headland penetrated by this tunnel. The Masseline

Harbour was completed after the war and opened in 1949. The use of either landing place is often dictated by wind and tide conditions. There is a third landing place known as Havre Gosselin on the western coast, sheltered by the nearby island of Brecqhou. The ascent from this is by steps and a steep path and is only possible on foot, bringing you to the top of the cliffs near the Pilcher Monument, a memorial to five men who were drowned in 1868 trying to reach Guernsey in an open boat in a storm. Near this landing place are the Gouliot Caves, with an incredible collection of Sea Anemones and other marine animals attached to their walls, which have earnt them the name of the 'Jewel Caves'. The descent to these on foot, down the chimney from the plateau is hazardous but well worth it at low tide. At certain states of the tide small fishing boats can take visitors into the caves by sea.

Little Sark is attached to Sark by a natural rock causeway known as La Coupée, about 100m long, some 80m (260ft.) above the sea and only about 3m wide at the top. This has a sheer drop on the eastern side, but it is possible to get down into Grande Grève on the western side by a steep path and many steps. Whilst on Little Sark be sure and make the descent to the Venus Pool and the Adonis Pool at opposite ends of the western extremity. In the crystal clear waters of these you may swim and watch the fish swimming below you amongst the waving many coloured seaweeds.

Sark has no cars but plenty of tractors, the roads are well kept, carefully graded gravel, forming a compacted surface known as macadam. They were kept up by the inhabitants each autumn, until the late 1950s, through an ancient Channel Island feudal custom known as *corvée*. Here every 'tenant' was required to give a number of days labour each year to keep the roads in good repair. This was considered as part of their rental dues and if the tenant was unable to perform the work, he paid someone to do it for him. They are now maintained by contractors paid for by Chief Pleas, the Sark Parliament, out of the various funds collected from Impôt duties on wines and spirits, the landing tax charged to visitors, etc. The roads lead to the Seigneurie the home of the island's hereditary ruler and most of the principal farms, bays, houses and hotels.

There are many footpaths branching off from them leading the pedestrian along field edges or across the commons and heathlands to the valleys and cliffs.

Starting from the harbour, Derrible Bay is to the south with lovely fine sand. From above there is an awe-inspiring view looking down into the Creux Derrible, a passage way and cave cut into the softer intrusion between two hard rocks over the millenia by the sea, whilst surface water, frost action and penetrating plant roots eventually caused the roof to fall in, created an opening at the surface. The headland the other side of the bay is the Hog's Back offering superb views along the coast. A path through the woods on the other side of this headland takes you down into Dixcart Bay with its natural stone arch. The sand here is partly overlain with a thin layer of small reddish grit. Return up the path to the Dixcart Hotel. If you have a map follow the cliff path from here to La Coupée.

On Little Sark you pass the ruins of the fort and come to Pot Bay which has a smaller cave known as 'The Pot', similar in formation to Creux Derrible. The old silver mines are on the cliff just above the Venus Pool. The main shaft is about 165m deep. The path continues along the western cliffs to the old mill and you will need to return along the road back to La Coupée.

Continuing up the western side, the privately owned island of Brecqhou is just offshore from the Gouliot Caves, with a narrow passage separating it from Sark. There is a fine view of Herm and Guernsey in the distance from here. Alderney can also be seen, to the north. There are a number of offshore stacks and tiny tidal islets along this stretch of the coast. At Port du Moulin, just below the Seigneurie there is a sheer drop of 80 metres to the beach below. Just beyond, a " Window" cut in the rock formerly allowed goods to be hauled up from the beach by a winch. Offshore are the three Autelets.

Just before the northern tip and the round tower, a path leads down to another set of caves Les Boutiques. They run right under the cliffs as a tunnel about 65m long with a vertical drop part way along, opening into a large hall like area, with another tunnel leading out the other side. These can be explored at low tide, but a powerful torch is advised if you wish to avoid the pools within and the vertical drop. On the eastern side of this headland is another small landing place, L'Epérquerie, a name which reminds us that conger eels and mackerel were dried here for export in mediaeval and Tudor times. There are more caves along this stretch including the Fairy Grotto, an area with two rock archways. A track beyond Creux Belet allows you to climb back up to Le Fort and a roadway back across the centre of the island, later turning out towards the cliffs again at La Colinette until you reach the path leading down to Point Robert Lighthouse. Built in 1912, perched halfway down the cliff, in 1994 this was finally automated and is now controlled from Alderney, the keepers being withdrawn at that time.

From Point Robert it is but a short distance along the coast back to the harbour, but you are well advised to return by the much longer way, along the road.

Most of the soil on Sark is acidic with a $p_H$ of about 6.5 on the top of the island, with a few areas as low as $p_H$ 5, whilst in some places along the base of the cliffs it rises to about $p_H$ 8.

# 4. HERM

Like Sark, Herm and Jethou are basically wave-cut platforms of harder rock, the comparatively shallow Little Russel Channel between them and Guernsey probably marking the line of a former river bed. Whilst Herm (about 1½ x ½ miles), 500 acres in extent at high tide, it is situated at 2° 27'W, 49° 28'N, which belongs to the States of Guernsey, has been leased from them since 1949 by Peter and (until her death in 1991), Jenny Wood and their family, is served by frequent boats from St. Peter Port and the public are welcomed, Jethou is still leased from the Crown by its tenant and is not open to the public. Starting either from the landing place at the harbour, which was built to serve the quarries mentioned at the end of the previous chapter, or the earlier landing place at Les Rosière steps, where the boat drops you depending on the tides, turn to the south and take the cliff path.

From the harbour the old Rosière Quarry, now the island's rubbish tip, is soon on your left. After passing the steps the path rises steeply to the most southerly point, Point Sauzebourge, reached after passing the old mine shaft on the rise above, almost buried in vegetation and not marked on the more recent maps. Evidence of neolithic occupation can be seen at several points along the way. The main plateau area about 65m or 200ft above sea level is above you to your left all along this path. Here the soil is slightly acid. There is a grand view of Guernsey and St. Peter Port all along this part of the island. In the early morning on a calm day you can hear the hum of traffic along Les Banques, a soothing thought for those enjoying the relaxation of a day out in Herm's peaceful surroundings and, far less attractively, one can often see the purple-brown haze of exhaust fumes along the coast road from St. Peter Port to St. Sampson. Again like Sark, there are no cars in Herm to disturb you or pollute the atmosphere. The visitor should beware on a sunny day, Herm's clear air allows plenty of UV light to pass and is very prone to giving the unwary a taste of sunburn.

Turning east from the point, the path stays along the clifftop with a few gaunt pine trees on the crest above you, around the highest point, about 71m (232ft). There are remnants of a number of Neolithic tombs along the way. Just before the most easterly point, as the path turns north again puffins nest in old rabbit burrows in the cliffs below you. The path descends gently to the top of Belvoir Bay, an attractive sandy cove where visiting yachts frequently anchor. Above the beach a welcoming café offers the opportunity to sit and admire the view. Toilets will be found a short way further along the path as you continue your walk. You have now come about half way round the island. Sark and Alderney are visible to the SE and NE respectively, and the French coast stretches all along the eastern horizon. There are a number of offshore rock stacks visible.

The path undulates and then descends sharply to another café and the start of the Shell Beach. This is backed by low mobile sand dunes, strengthened in recent years by the planting of marram and other stabilising plants.

The Shell Beach, its half-mile length unique in its formation within the British Isles, has been exploited by collectors and ornament and souvenir makers from Victorian times. Today only the commoner species are generally found, but then the beach contained many shells of molluscs no longer to be found in northern latitudes. These are presumably remnants of the sub-tropical conditions of the Cambrian period when the coal measures were laid down. Another theory has been advanced that the shells may have been swept up here in more recent times by strong currents from the south and south-west.

The flat area of Herm Common, forming almost a square bounded on three sides by the sea, has a number of Neolithic remains, an obelisk in the middle of the northern edge, replacing a menhir destroyed by the stone quarriers in the 19th century, some interesting plants, including areas so densely covered with the flat-growing, spiny, white-flowered Burnet Rose as to make sitting down uncomfortable, and an excellent selection of birds and butterflies to be seen in season. On the western side a small rocky eminence known as La Petite Monceaux has a marshy area, with acidic soil and a small pond, surrounded by willows, at its foot. Elsewhere on the Common, the soil is slightly alkaline due to the shell content and this enables calcicole plants like the Burnet Rose and Salad Burnet to thrive in this area.

The path continues along past the Cemetery, through a grove of trees and past the camping site, the village with its shops and Mermaid Tavern, back to the harbour and the White House Hotel. From here a steep road through thick woodland takes you to the top of the island. Unusually, amongst the trees here are many clumps of Butcher's Broom, a dark green spiky plant usually only found on open cliffs and heaths, which bears its minute white flowers and large scarlet berries on modified flattened stems called cladodes, which serve the plant in place of leaves. The Manoir, Farm and the Chapel of St. Tugual are on the high plateau at the top of this road. Here the soil, as in the other islands is slightly acidic. From the cross roads here another road runs along the spine of the island between the cultivated fields and a track descends on the other side to Belvoir Bay.

Jethou, just offshore from Herm is about 600m across, whilst Crevichon, a little way from that is only about 3 acres in extent.

# PALÆONTOLOGY

The few fossils found in the Bailiwick have nearly all been washed up on the beaches from offshore deposits of chalk or limestone.

*Guernsey*

Guernsey having no sedimentary rocks has nothing recorded other than the specimens from this source. These few specimens are principally echinoids (Sea Urchins) and water-worn fossils about 2in. or more long, (about the size of a rifle bullet), of the 'guard' of the Belemnite, an extinct Cephalopod resembling an octopus. Flint nodules are also found occasionally.

Various mollusc shells have been found in limey nodules at the bottom of the loess deposits.

*Alderney*

Despite its considerable quantity of the sedimentary sandstone, few fossils have been recorded from Alderney either. No fossil imprints or remains, have ever been recorded from the sandstone deposits.

There are some local specimens in the Museum geological case, which include; various echinoids; one, unidentified, from the Jurassic Period; a crinoid; an echinocorys; and an echinus. A Bijocian bivalve and a Compound Coral.

A small Brachiopod was found in a flint nodule from the Longis peat beds in 1977 and a cretaceous period Echinoid embedded in flint was found nearby in 1982. Many quite large, water-worn flint nodules and the occasional unworn one with chalk still adhering to it, have been found along Longis beach. The inclusions sometimes noted in these are usually found to be mineral, rather than animal in origin.

A piece of calcareous material bearing the imprint of part of the outer curve of an Ammonite about 6in. in diameter was found on Longis beach a few years ago and in 1988 a section about 9in. long of a very large grey coral showing excellent internal structure was found in the same area. Both of these and the flints must have originated in offshore chalk deposits.

Belemnites may often be found amongst the gravel on Platte Saline. One presumes these to have come from a similar site to the large flint nodules also found from time to time and the considerable quantity of small, porous, water-worn, 'pebbles' of calcareous material found here.

*Sark* and *Herm* also have no sedimentary rocks and seem to be lacking in fossilised remains other than the rare, water-borne, ones recorded above.

*Chapter 3*

# THE SETTLEMENT OF THE ISLANDS

Historians have traditionally relied to a great extent on previously published material for their sources and as a consequence many major aspects, for example, the colonisation or settlement of the islands, the evolution of field systems and names and their economic and agricultural development, have not been thoroughly explored. At the same time this reliance has perpetuated a history including legend and fable, bogus documents and family trees through the plagiarism of unreliable material. During the German occupation of Alderney from 1940-45, virtually all of the island's records disappeared and present day historians have to carry out much patient research for original contemporary material in archives, libraries and museums in the other Channel Islands, France and the U.K. and in the Public Record Office in England.

The Channel Islands form a well defined geographical group with obvious physical and cultural links with the mainland of present day Normandy and Brittany, but, in the past, little comparison has been made between them with the evolution of the other islands in the archipelago, or with the influence of events in and the culture of, Normandy, whilst the effects of the link with the English Crown in historic times, have been the primary concern.

Flint tools dating from about 150,000 years ago have been found at various sites. These are presumably the remaining evidence of the small bands of hunter-gatherers who roamed the continent at this time when the area was probably largely deciduous forest.

Guernsey at one time was reported to have 68 dolmens, of which only about 15 have survived and 39 menhirs, in addition to the promontory fort at Jerbourg. Several of the Megalithic passage graves are now well preserved and open for inspection. In particular Le Creux ès Faies on the coast near Lihou Island, La Varde on L'Ancresse Common and Le Déhus, at Paradis in the Vale. This last is one of the finest passage graves in NW Europe and has a unique human figure holding a bow incised underneath one of its capstones. These are well worth a visit.

There are several other dolmens on L'Ancresse Common, and also what is probably the oldest stone structure in Europe and, at more than 7,000 years old, possibly in the world. Known as Les Fouillages, it is more than 1,000 years older than the Pyramids. Over 30,000 artefacts were recovered from the site when it was excavated between 1979 and 1981. These suggested use of the site and possibly occupation of the area over a period of nearly 4,000 years. Many of the finds, including several exquisite flint arrow heads, are now on display in the Guernsey Museum and Art Gallery at Candie in St. Peter Port.

La Varde and three other megaliths were first described by Joshua Gosselin in a paper in *Archaeologica* in 1811. Later, during the period from the 1830s to about 1870, several members of the Lukis family excavated and recorded many of the Bailiwick sites and set up a museum at their house in The Grange. The father, F.C. Lukis (1788-1871) recorded their activities both in the Bailiwick and elsewhere, in six large manuscript volumes entitled *Collectanea Antiqua*, which are now kept at the Guernsey Museum and Art Gallery, together with many detailed drawings and their huge collection of artefacts, bequeathed in 1907 to the States of Guernsey by his son Francis. Alderney excavations are recorded in volume five of this work.

In Alderney the oldest remains of human occupation are probably the large double Neolithic dolmen know as Les Porciaux, above Longis Common and the tiny dolmen Roc à L'Epine on the hillside above Fort Tourgis, both probably dating from around 4,500-4,000BC. In March 1983 a wooden spear, which has been dated to approximately 4,000BC and in 1991 another wooden spear shaft of about the same age, were found in the peat beds at Longis. The first is on display in the Museum. Both of these are from a period not long after Alderney became an island. A stone axe dated between 3,500 and 2,500BC was found at L' Emauve in 1986 and a flat bronze axe head, from about 2,000BC, was found in the same area. There is a large stone circle at Mannez and the remains of two others on Les Rochers.

Sark, which was probably separated from Guernsey at about the same time as Alderney became an island, appears to have had as many as ten dolmens in the early 19th century, but by 1875 only two remained more or less complete. These are both on Little Sark. Stone, copper and bronze axes have also been found in the island. Some thirty stone axes and a number of anvil stones and mullers have also been found, many are now in the Guernsey Museum, together with a number of stone rings, probably spindle whorls of Gallo-Roman date. These are of a design unique to Sark, known as "rouettes de faïteaux" or fairy rings. There also appears to have been a promontory fort on the northern tip of the island, cut off by a ditch and earthworks from the main part of the island.

There are the remains of at least a dozen cists or graves on the higher parts of Herm and several more on the common, with some menhirs and a stone circle. Like Alderney, Herm was thought at one time to have been used by ancient peoples, simply as a burial place, but occupation by man is proved by the number of worked flints which have been found there. From a much later period there are the remains of an early 11th century Augustinian Priory.

Jethou holds the remains of several cromlechs, possibly three menhirs and a stone circle.

The islands taken together, have a residue of megalithic culture which is quite disproportionate to their size, but the reasons for this have not yet been fully explored, nor has its subsequent influence on the settlement of the islands. It has been suggested that they were regarded as *Holy Islands* and that some of the dead were brought to them for burial, from nearby Normandy or Brittany. There are legends about this in each of the islands and also in Normandy. The time scales involved were, until quite recently, a matter of informed guesswork and the period between the estimated dates of the various monuments, has often been thought to be barren.

In Guernsey many of these were destroyed for building stone, but many more have survived, been excavated and several put into a condition where they can be visited. The reader is referred to the several works on the archaeology of the Bailiwick for greater detail.

Unfortunately in Alderney, expediency, at the various periods of building of defensive works in the island has resulted in most of the megalithic graves having their capstones broken up and removed for building purposes, since it was easier to build a fire under them to crack the stone than to quarry new stone, whilst many of the uprights were left in situ, because it was too troublesome to dig them out. The very sites chosen for these defence works were often and logically, the sites previously occupied by earlier cultures, effectively destroying most of the evidence. The possible existence of promontory forts on Roselle Point and Essex Hill was thus almost entirely obscured.

The uneducated nature of both landowners and workers, in former times, contributed largely to a total lack of appreciation of the value and historical significance of what was being destroyed.

In the last forty years or so, the development of radio-carbon dating methods and the use of pollen analysis, has had a great influence on the accurate dating of those structures remaining and has contributed to the preparation of an accurate chronology of prehistoric times. Not much of this radio-carbon dating work has yet been carried out in the Channel Islands, but the peat samples from each of the islands' few known peat deposits, have been carefully studied and classified.

The work that has been done on the monuments of nearby Brittany by Dr. P.R. Giot and others, has shown that the Megalithic culture and agricultural methods were well established there before 3,000BC and by comparison of the structures raised, probably in the islands also. Studies on raised beaches and the changing sea levels have established that, in more recent times, there were marked rises in the sea level around 1,200BC and again around AD500 and this offers an explanation for the existence of megalithic remains, especially those found in Jersey, below the present high water mark. Coastal erosion has also played a part in this process and in particular the graves discovered near the Nunnery in Alderney, around the turn of this century and also in the 1920s - 30s, were probably, in that earlier time, some distance from the present shore.

The Bronze Age was possibly brought about by the spreading of small groups of skilled metal workers across Europe, bringing their new skills to the existing population, who were users of stone and flint tools, rather than by any wholesale movement of a different race. Large numbers of Bronze Age implements and weapons have been found, including the famous Alderney Hoard of some 200 items found just above Longis Common in 1832, now to be seen in the Guernsey Museum. Other bronze weapons and Iron Age pottery and implements from this area are on display in the Alderney Museum.

An early Iron Age site on the western edge of Longis common, dated to 490BC by the charcoal found there, with a considerable pottery manufacturing area, was excavated in 1968-70 by Ken and Peggy Wilson, curators of the Alderney Museum, at Les Huguettes, about 100m NW of the Nunnery, in an area known in the 1830s as the "Potter's Field". Some 40 pots, a bronze razor and tweezers and some loom weights and spindles were recovered and several are now exhibited in the Alderney Museum.

The Bronze Age was followed by a more positive movement of Iron Age Celts, or Gauls, a tall, fair, blue-eyed, war-like race, who started to move westward from beyond the Danube in the eighth century BC and reached the Cotentin some 4-500 years later. Theirs was a different culture, language and religion, they built seaworthy ships of oak, which would have enabled them to reach the islands easily and wooden houses. They cultivated the soil, bringing wheat, oats, barley, rye and beans, with them. Their priests were an educated class who served a long noviciate, the *Druids*, whose religion involved animal and human sacrifice. Their dominance in the region lasted about 500 years until they were conquered by the Romans.

Until quite recently, Alderney was thought to be the only island with any definite and proven evidence of Roman presence, but in the last twenty years, considerable evidence of Roman culture, has been found in the other islands, whilst a Roman shipwreck excavated and recovered from St. Peter Port harbour and the excavation of a Roman settlement at La Plaiderie, close to the harbour, has helped to establish the existence of a well defined trade route from SW France and Spain to Britain, especially Dorset, particularly through Guernsey with its superb natural anchorage and Alderney, rather than through Jersey. The discovery in 1718 of the "Sark Hoard" of 13 engraved or embossed silver gilt phalera either about 7cm or 15cm across, together with 18 other pieces, in an earthenware pot bound with iron hoops, probably of the 1st century BC, also indicates Roman occupation of that island. The hoard vanished sometime later, but fortunately a detailed set of

8m Raised Beach on Burhou

Dolerite vein at Bibette Head Alderney

Hedgehog

One of Alderney's Blond Hedgehogs

Sandhill Snails on Sea Kale

Black Slug

Goose Barnacles on a piece of floating timber

Stalked Sea Anemone

Sea Hares

Dog Whelk & Acorn Barnacles

Ormer grazing on seaweeds

Emperor Moth and Caterpillar

Cinnabar Moth and Caterpillar on Ragwort

38

Jersey Tiger Moth

Swallow tail Moth

Common Blues mating

Small Copper Butterfly

Hoverfly (Volucella)

Cockchafer Beetle

Dead Man's Fingers fungus

Tulostoma brumale. Note pore on top

Bell-shaped Mottlegill on horse dung

Giant Puffball

Orange Peel fungus

Jew's Ear fungus

Parasol Mushroom

Dacrymyces on Gorse stem

Lichens on a seashore rock

Lichens in a quarry

Male fruiting cups on the liverwort Marchantia

Female receptacles of Marchantia

A Sea Mat on Laminaria

Dead Man's Fingers in Gouliot Caves

Breadcrumb Sponges in Gouliot Caves

Beadlet Anemones

Star Ascidian etc.

Channelled Wrack (Pelvetia)

Sea Thong (Himanthalia). Note perennial 'buttons'

A pressed specimen of Peacock's Tail Seaweed (Padina)

drawings of the objects, drawn by George Vertue in 1725 was found this century, loose in a volume which was purchased by the Society of Antiquaries in 1741. This has enabled them to be more accurately identified and dated.

The next great movement across Europe was of the German tribes from beyond the Rhine. Clovis and his Franks defeated the Romans in AD 486, the Emperor made him Consul and he became master of Gaul, which was renamed Francia. Clovis became a Christian in 496, honouring a promise he had made if he defeated the Romans, but his conquest did not significantly alter the language and customs of the region. When he died in 511, his kingdom was divided between his sons and the Channel Islands became part of the province of Neustria.

The introduction of Christianity to the islands around the fifth - sixth centuries, coincided with its period of rapid expansion across Western Europe within the limits of the well organised social structure of the Roman Empire.

From about the year 800, Scandinavian or *Viking* pirates and robbers made periodic raids on the islands each summer. Alderney with its small, poor, population would not have provided as great an attraction to raiders as the larger, wealthier islands of Jersey and Guernsey, which suffered much rape, pillage and burning and probable robbing of some of the Neolithic tombs, but it was perhaps at this time that the settlement of St. Marie (now St. Anne) developed, partly hidden in the central lower hollow of the island, away from the attentions of coastal raiders, to whom the settlement at Longis would have been exposed. The monks from St. Magloire's monastery in Sark, established in 565, were driven out by the Vikings in 840, but returned later and remained there until 1463. The saint's cell still exists in part in the Seigneurie gardens, but little trace of any other monastic structure earlier than mediaeval date exists.

Many of today's place names for coastal and offshore features of the islands derive from the Norse language of these sea raiders or Northmen, but few of the names for inland features in the three smaller islands have these roots, tending to confirm the theory that there was little penetration inland, a slightly different situation from the larger islands of Guernsey and Jersey.

The advance of the Northmen was so irresistible, that by 878, King Alfred in England was forced to surrender half of the kingdom to the Danes and in 911, by the Treaty of St. Claire-sur-Epte, Charles the Simple of France conceded the ecclesiastical province of Rouen and half the province of Francia, to their leader, Rollo, with committal powers as 'Count' of the region. The Cotentin and the Islands were not included at this time, but were later secured by his son William Longsword, about 933, who continued the westward expansion.

In the second half of the 10th century homage was performed for the region to the Duke of Francia. Rollo's grandson, Richard I styled himself *Marquis of the*

Normans and referred to his 'kingdom'. In 1015 when the Duchy of Francia was re-absorbed into the Kingdom of the Franks, he assumed the title of *Duke of Normandy*. Richard II styled himself 'Duke and Patrician' and claimed the right to control the church in his Duchy and the appointment of inferior Counts. The parish boundaries in Guernsey were probably established about this time as the boundaries of the separate Fiefs thus created. In Alderney there was only ever a single parish where the church was dedicated to Our Lady, although a number of Frairies *(see note on page 52)* dedicated to other saints existed until the dissolution of the monasteries by Henry VIII.

The language of all the islands until the present century was Norman-French with a local patois differing slightly between each island, even between the 'high' and 'low' parishes in Jersey and Guernsey. Legal documents and property deeds, continued to be written in French until the middle of the present century, whilst Court proceedings were conducted and the Billets d'Etats for States meetings were still in French, or from the 1920s often in both English and French until 1948 in Alderney and a little later in Guernsey.

If present sea levels fell by only 15-20m Jersey would be reunited with France. Another 10-15m fall would join Alderney to the land mass thus created, with only a shallow channel separating it from the, by then, larger island formed from Guernsey, Herm and Sark. A total fall of 50-60m would form a solid land mass from a few miles north of the Cap de la Hague, extending about 20 miles westward and then south to join up at Cap Finisterre and re-establish the situation shown in Figure 5.

Alderney, because of its small population, experienced a far greater influence from Britain over the centuries from mediaeval times than the larger islands, especially in relation to the need to defend them in the 16th to 19th centuries, principally from fear of attack by the French. The huge, (in relation to its indigenous population numbers), intermittent influx of workmen and troops for this purpose caused a greater use of English at an earlier stage than in the other islands. The resulting fortifications built at different times, have exerted a long term influence on the ecology of the island and no doubt introduced many new species of plants and insects, either deliberately or inadvertently. This was further affected by the Germans, whose vast complex of fortifications, built by thousands of slaveworkers during the Second World War, cover large tracts of both Guernsey and Alderney.

The remaining Norman-French language of the people of Alderney virtually disappeared with the almost total evacuation of the population in 1940. In Sark a large proportion of the population remained, in Jersey about three-quarters and in Guernsey half, so that the language is still heard in those islands, although principally amongst the older inhabitants. Societies exist there to promote its continued use.

Despite the number of Neolithic remains on Sark and the monastery mentioned above, abandoned in 1463, little is known about its mediaeval history or population. The apparently uninhabited island was occupied by the French for a few years from 1549 until they were evicted by a Spanish force in 1553. The Emperor Charles offered to sell the island back to Queen Mary I, she refused to pay and the Spanish forces were withdrawn a few months later. The island was again uninhabited for about ten years until in 1563, Queen Elizabeth issued a patent to a Jerseyman, Helier de Carteret who had offered to defend the island against any further invasion by the French. He was granted the fee-farm on the understanding that he would maintain not less than 40 men-at-arms there at all times to defend it. He did this by creating 40 tenancies, each of which was alloted to a family, mostly from Jersey. In 1572, the Queen rewarded him for repopulating and defending the island by declaring it an independent fief of the crown. Since that time the island has been ruled by the descendants of de Carteret and their assigns, and to this day, the owners of the 40 tenancies each hold a seat by right in Chief Pleas, the island's parliament.

In the 18th century, religious persecution of protestants and later the French Revolution, caused a huge exodus of Huguenots and emigrés to the islands which had a considerable effect on the practise of Christianity in them. In the 19th and early 20th century, British government building works and garrisons also created a large addition to the populations, many of those involved marrying into local families and remaining afterwards. Since the Second World War large numbers of expatriate British, returning from former colonies, have made their homes here and the islands' low tax status have attracted many others from the UK. In the last twenty years the rapid development of the finance industry, especially in Jersey and Guernsey has caused another large influx of predominantly young people, once again affecting the culture and economy of the islands.

A number of these people have brought plants (and probably associated insects) from their former homes also affecting the flora and fauna. Many of these will undoubtedly become naturalised in time, indeed some have already become so.

The different times at which the several islands of the archipelago became separated from continental Europe and later from each other, account in some degree for the differences in their flora and fauna. The number of plant species found in each island reduces proportionately to their reducing size. A similar decrease is noted in birds and insects, whilst several land animals, being totally restricted in their distribution to those which were present before the separations occurred and those which have been subsequently introduced by man, differ in a number of minor respects from similar species in England or France.

NOTE:

The Frairies or 'brotherhoods' were opposed by the church until the Twelfth Century, after which they were charged with the upkeep of the chapels or churches and the distribution of alms. By mediæval times they were a fraternity of people who, wishing to secure perpetual acts of intercession after their death, to save their souls from purgatory, by the recitation of masses and prayers, contributed to a common *Obit fund* and entered into an agreement with a local hermit or a priest for this purpose and to cover their burial expenses. Legacies were left for the support of the church or these chapels, more often in the form of a wheat-rent or perpetual charge on some family property, or by donating a small piece of real property, money at that time being little used in Alderney. The members of the Frairies met annually at their chapel on the feast day of its patron saint.

They were destroyed and their revenues were confiscated by the Crown, at the time of the Reformation.

Roberts' Cross Dolmen on Herm

*Chapter 4*

# THE WILDLIFE OF THE ISLANDS

### Introduction.

The Flora and Fauna of the Channel Islands is influenced in its relationship to that of mainland Britain and France by two principal factors.

Firstly, as has already been noted, the period of time since the various islands in the group became detached from the Continent and from each other, which has limited the range of plants and animals present in each island.

Secondly, perhaps more particularly with regard to the flora, the effect of strong, salt-laden winds across small islands and their exposed situation. This is especially true of Alderney, the only island actually in the English Channel, and thus not screened to any great extent from the east and south. Rabbits have also restricted the growth of tree seedlings throughout the islands.

During the time between the last ice age and the present day, vast forests, with oak predominating, but including alder, hazel, lime, myrtle and elm, with some pine, covered the islands and much of present day France. Evidence of this lies in several peat beds around Jersey and Guernsey and in a small area of Alderney, sometimes exposed at freak tides and after storms, which have on several occasions this century revealed tree stumps.

It is likely that much of the forest was cleared for crop growing during the Bronze Age, or burnt during the Iron Age and the exhaustion of the timber supply, or a freak inundation by blown sand, are possible reasons for the apparently sudden cessation of use of several ancient inhabited sites. Any large animals such as Wild Ox, Deer and Boars, which might have roamed the area when the islands were still attached to mainland Europe would have been eliminated by hunting by this time. It may also account for the comparative lack of trees on the smaller Islands, which was sufficiently noticeable to cause John Leland (1506-1552), to note on his sketch map of the Channel Islands, 'Alderney is fairly fertile in corn and cattle, but is notably lacking in trees', a comment echoed by Ansted in his "Channel Islands", (1862), who states that 'Alderney and Sark are very badly provided with trees'.

In Britain and the larger Channel Islands, from Elizabethan times onwards, much of the Common Lands were gradually enclosed, effectively denying the local inhabitants traditional grazing and other rights. Sark was divided into 40 tenancies when the abandoned island was repopulated from Jersey in Elizabethan times, a situation which still exists today. The cultivated areas in the islands expanded as the population increased and, because of the limited amount of land available, were continuously cultivated, the fertility being maintained by the annual application of large amounts of *vraic* (seaweed). This also helped in retaining moisture in the predominantly sandy and often quite thin soils. Apart from the Crown or Seigneurial lands, retained in Alderney until 1830 when most of it was divided amongst the inhabitants, the land was not enclosed there and was still farmed on the communal open field system until 1940. Even today there are few boundary walls or fences on the Blayes.

Most of what was consumed on each island was grown there until recent years and local cattle provided both milk and meat, gradually developing by continuous inbreeding and later laws restricting the import of cattle from other places, into the two distinct Jersey and Guernsey Breeds, with Alderney and Sark cattle being closely allied to the Guernsey breed.

Whilst agriculture and horticulture have thrived in the two larger islands and Sark and today still form a substantial part of their economies, in Alderney, compared with 50 years ago very little of the island is regularly cultivated and where the poorer areas were regularly grazed by cattle and sheep 100 years ago, today much is covered by bramble, bracken and gorse. The practise of cutting gorse for fuel, particularly for bread ovens, has also virtually ceased throughout the islands and much of the gorse is old, leaving the new shoots to gradually surround dead wood. For centuries in Guernsey most farms owned furzebrakes on the cliffs from which they cut their fuel and in Alderney the inhabitants had been allowed to graze stock and cut bracken and gorse on the crown or common lands until they were divided up.

In the following chapters we will look in turn at each of the several groups of plants and animals to be found in the Bailiwick in the wild today.

Furze near the old Silver Mine on Little Sark

*Chapter 5*

# THE PLANTS

The known flora of Guernsey today contains about 1,200 species of flowering plants and ferns, whilst Alderney has about 800. By comparison, Sark has about 600, Herm 400, Brecqhou 295, Jethou 185, Lihou 120 and Crevichon 52, whilst Jersey has about 1,500. In all the islands a number of them were probably introduced accidentally by the army during Victorian times, plants like the Hottentot Fig being especially prevalent in the vicinity of the various forts. Each of the four principal islands contain a small number of species which have not, as yet, been recorded in the others.

Visitors and residents alike are urged neither to pick the flowers of, nor to uproot, any of these plants. Gathering of blackberries and rose hips in season is of course acceptable.

Let us first look at the lower plants.

## ALGAE

Whilst the Marine Algal flora of Guernsey has been updated several times, no satisfactory list of the freshwater algae, or the seaweeds of Alderney or Sark has been published since that in Marquand's *Flora*, with some later additions in the Annual Botanical reports in *Transactions*. The overall picture is not significantly different from that of the Channel and Atlantic coasts of England. The islands as a whole need an up-to-date survey, as much of the nomenclature used in those early lists is now out-of-date.

### Marine Algae

The development of the seaweeds usually found in a given area depends on six main factors;

(i) the average water temperature and its variation throughout the year, (which affects their geographical distribution). In the Bailiwick over the period 1980-94, the mean warmest sea temperature was 16.5°, reached in week 36 (beginning of September), and the coldest 8.25° in weeks 8 & 9, (the last two weeks in February). Round Alderney the figures were often about a degree lower;

(ii) whether the substrate is sandy or rocky and the presence or absence of tidal pools. In the summer, pools, particularly those on the upper shore, can heat up considerably and their salinity increase through evaporation;

(iii) the degree of desiccation and the temperatures they can withstand whilst exposed between tides, (the actual duration of exposure at any given point of course varies greatly between spring and neap tides);

(iv) their ability to withstand wave action, (i.e. whether the coast is exposed or sheltered),

(v) the light intensity and daily duration they need to grow and reproduce, (which largely affects the depth of water in which they can survive and the latitudes in which they grow); and;

(vi) the salinity of the water at their place of growth, (this can also vary considerably in estuaries or where fresh water runs across a cliff or beach).

In more recent years sea pollution has also become an important factor in the development and distribution of a number of species of marine organisms, including the algae.

A brief list of the more common seaweed species to be found round the islands is given here, in the sequence of their usual zonation from the upper shore downwards to shallow wading depth below the lowest water mark of spring tides. The actual species found on any shore around the islands will depend on the degree of exposure to wave action, the steepness of the shore and the relative proportions of rock/sand/shingle.

**Splash Zone;** exposed for most of the time.

Channelled Wrack or *Pelvetia;* found in a narrow zone at normal HWM or in the splash zone on exposed shores, often in a very much reduced moss-like form. Do not confuse these patches with the similar appearing growth of the tufted lichen *Lichina pygmaea,* which is sometimes seen from just below the Pelvetia, down to mid-tide level. This lichen harbours a rich fauna of small, even minute, crustaceans, insects and molluscs. Look particularly for the red bivalve, *Lassea rubra,* 1.5-2mm long.

**Upper shore;** exposed for up to eight hours in each tide; this and the next zone, combined, are sometimes called the **Fucus zone.**

Next comes Spiral Wrack; with Laver forming a thin dark red/purplish coating over exposed rocks in sandy areas. A type of bread can be made with this. The bright green flat fronds of Sea Lettuce, also a species formerly frequently used for food; and thin green hollow tubes of *Enteromorpha intestinalis* are found on rocks and in shallow pools in this area, especially where there is fresh water seepage. They occur on most beaches;

**Middle shore;** exposed for four to six hours at each tide.

Bladder Wrack, with, a little further down, Toothed Wrack, and Knotted Wrack, both frequently having bright red tufts of *Polysiphonia lanosa* attached to them.

The pools in this zone hold a wide variety of green, red and brown algae. Most easily recognised are the pinky-white calcareous clumps of Corallina, of which there are several species, encrusting the edges of the pools. These provide homes amongst their branches for more minute animal species. Pink or violet chalky, somewhat knobbly encrustation on the rock sides are *Lithothamnion* and *Lithophyllum* species. Irish Moss or Carrageen and the similar looking *Gigartina stellata,* often gathered with it, are common in these pools particularly towards LWM. Their flat, reddish-purple, dichotomously branched cartilaginous fronds are edible, either cooked or raw, and make a nutritious pudding, frequently made in Guernsey during the last war. Gelatin can be extracted from them. Pointed red, round, dichotomously branched stems of *Furcellaria lubricalis* and the fairly similar round-ended stems of *Polyides rotundus* will be also be found here.

Easily identified are the dull, dark-green fronds of *Codium tomentosum,* similar in shape but larger than the previous two species. Soft much-branched, fine-stemmed clumps of several green *Spongomorpha,* and *Cladophora* species and the olive-green *Enteromorpha* species are not always easy to distinguish from each other.

The reader should again refer to one of the specialised guides to help sort out the many dozens of beautiful seaweeds found in these pools and those on the lower shore.

**Lower shore;** exposed for one to four hours each tide.

Brown seaweeds here include; Sea Oak, common in pools in this region with its pod-like float bladders; the continuously forked *Bifurcaria bifurcata;* brightly green/blue iridescent (when submerged), much branched bushy plants of the Bladder Weed and flat, dark spotted, olive green, leaf-like fronds of *Punctaria plantaginea,* are all easy to spot.

**Sub-littoral zone;** not generally exposed at all.

Oarweed, this lies flat on the rock or water surfaces at extreme low tide; Sea Belt, or Dabberlocks, which gets its Latin name *Laminaria saccharina,* from the white sugary powder, mannitol, which appears on its surface as it dries. *Alaria esculenta,* a thin ribbon-like Laminarian with a thickened midrib, is eaten as a salad in some coastal areas. It is more frequently found on exposed coasts. Sea Bootlace, with a thin, tough, unbranched, hollow stem up to 4-5m long and Thongweed, its dichotomously branched flattened stems growing afresh each year up to 2-3m. long, from a small round perennial, button-like holdfast. These and the flat, soft, olive-green fronds of *Dictyota dichotoma* are the principal brown seaweeds found in this zone, often with epiphtic red seaweeds growing on them, Dulse, another of the seaweeds used as food and the pink fronds, like chains of beads, of *Lomentaria articulata* being the most frequent on the Fucoids and Laminarians. Look particularly in this area for the beautiful fan-like fronds of the Peacock's Tail. Up to 10cm long these are curved and have a lime-green inner surface and are brown with green stripes on the outer side of the curve.

Another brown seaweed found entangled with the kelps, and often cast up on the shore is *Desmarestia aculeata,* with soft spines looking a bit like a Hawthorn twig, it frequently bears epiphytic, small balloon-like, soft spongy, brown masses of *Leathesia difformis.*

At greater depths, the huge palmate fronds, up to 3.5m. long of *Laminaria hyperborea* with several red epiphytes occur. These have a much branched holdfast and a rough round stipe and remain erect at extreme low spring tides, often standing up out of the water, whilst of a similar general appearance and even larger size, up to 4.5m., *Saccharina polyschides* has a large (up to 10cm.), thick, round, hollow, knobbly holdfast and a flattened wavy-edged stipe. They are often washed up after a storm.

The Laminarians define the limits of the sub-littoral zone.

Japanese Oarweed, *Sargassum muticum,* an invasive newcomer, the long branched fronds of which, floating in patches, can cause considerable problems by wrapping themselves round the propellor shafts of ships and motor cruisers, is gradually appearing round our coasts especially near the harbours.

The lists above represent only a small part of the littoral zone algae to be found by the careful observer, who can spend many happy hours studying them in the rock pools which abound in some part of all of the islands' bays.

The zonation on primarily sandy shores or on shingle is somewhat different and although there is usually a rich fauna, the intertidal area is often pretty barren of algae, apart from driftweed along the strand line. In the splash zone just in front of dune areas, a number of flowering plants will be found growing in the sand or small shingle. Marram, Sand and Sea Couch-grasses, Sea Kale, Sea Beet, Sea Spurge, Spear-leaved and Babington's Orache, Prickly Saltwort, Sea Rocket, Sea Sandwort, Yellow Horned-poppy, Sea Bindweed, Sand Sedge and Buck's-horn Plantain being the commonest.

In summer Sea Lettuce and *Enteromorpha* will be noticed in the flat, shallow wet areas towards the bottom of the tide, especially if there is freshwater seepage in this area. *Zostera,* another flowering plant, is found in the sublittoral zone off several parts of the coasts, usually above the Laminarians, particularly where there is a muddy substrate.

**Freshwater Algae**

Marquand's book and lists record some 44 species and 9 Desmids from Guernsey, where he commented that they were "but meagrely represented". There seems to be no record of any investigation in Alderney until the present authors, who have looked very superficially at the species most likely to be seen without the aid of a microscope, most of which can at least be identified with a good hand lens and we have also made a brief microscopic examination of the water from several widely separated permanent surface sources. No lists have been found for the smaller islands

Of the terrestrial species, the almost ubiquitous *Pleurococcus vulgaris* is regularly encountered on tree trunks, wooden fences and damp shady walls and *Protococcus viridis* is found in similar situations. Look also in this situation for the bright orange-red colour of *Chroolepus aureus,* which, despite its colour, is a member of the Chlorophyceae or green algae. On the ground, especially at the base of damp walls, look for the pinky-red patches, looking like blood stains of *Porphyridium cruentum,* also a green alga.

Single-celled Blue-green algae (Myxophyceae or Cyanophyceae) sometimes appear in domestic ponds and give the water a bloom like pea soup. This rapidly deoxygenates the water and can cause the death of the fish if not dealt with promptly. Species of *Anaboena* which form beadlike chains of minute cells without a proper nucleus or chloroplast are most commonly involved. Very occasionally this can cause problems in reservoirs or other larger bodies of water.

In ponds, domestic pools and quarries most of the species present are microscopic, but the more obvious threads of the several filamentous green algae can be seen with the naked eye. Long, fine, dark-green, tangled, unbranched threads of *Spirogyra* species will sometimes be noted, the spiral arrangement of the contents of each individual cell can usually be distinguished with a good hand lens. Cells have a proper nucleus and the green colouring or chlorophyll is organised into chloroplasts. Similar in outward appearance, *Zygnema* is slightly constricted between cells and the cell contents are usually grouped into star-shaped clusters, whilst *Cladophora* has branched filaments with short spiky clusters of branchlets on the main filaments. Collectively or singly, these and other species may form dense yellow-green patches of Blanket Weed or 'Cot', which fill with air bubbles, break loose from the substrate and float to the surface, in warm sunny weather. In Alderney this is especially noticeable on Longis pond in mid-summer. They frequently invade small garden ponds and can become a pest which is difficult to eradicate. The cell walls have a very high silica content and after removing from the pond and piling into heaps can take many months to rot.

Filaments of *Microspora* are to be found in small stagnant patches and pools and in drinking troughs.

Of the microscopic green species, *Chlamydomonas* with its twin flagellae on the pear-shaped cell, *Eudorina,* spherical with many flagellae all over, colonies of *Volvox* which form a beautiful hollow sphere, each individual member of which has two short flagella which beat continuously and spin the sphere slowly. *Euglena* has a slipper-shaped cell and one flagellum. They are all quite easy to recognise under the microscope although there are usually several species of each genus. The single-celled *Chlorella* can also turn pond water green, but without the harmful effect of the *Cyanophyceae*.

Many species of colourless Diatoms or green Desmids appear in most pond and stream water samples when examined under a powerful microscope. Charophytes may be found in some waters.

## THE LARGER FUNGI
## (MUSHROOMS & TOADSTOOLS)

Marquand recorded 612 species of fungi from Guernsey, with the aid of a mycologist from Kew Gardens; he also recorded 109 from Alderney and 13 from Lihou. He does not seem to have noted them in the other islands. Notes of various specimens found in the islands from time to time appear in the annual Botany Section reports in *Transactions*. Two large articles on the Microfungi of the Bailiwick in 1981 and the larger Fungi in 1989 provide the most recent information. In a 2 week foray in 1989, Watling recorded 76 macro and 44 microspecies from Guernsey, 23 and 25 from Sark, 38 and 14 from Herm and 1 from Lihou. As Alderney is poorly supplied with large woodland areas, the species of larger gill, pore and bracket, fungus normally found in this habitat are, not surprisingly, in short supply.

The more commonly seen macro-species are;

Field and Horse mushrooms, although these do not seem to be that common in Guernsey; The Prince, (all *Agaricus* spp.); Parasol and Shaggy Parasol, (*Lepiota* spp.); Common Inkcap and Shaggy Inkcap, (*Coprinus* spp.); Wood Blewit and Field Blewit, (*Lepista* spp.); Honey Fungus, various Boletus, Russula and Clitocybe species, several small Puffballs, (*Lycoperdon, Bovista* and *Calvatia* spp.); and Giant Puffballs, (*Langermannia gigantea*). These last grow in damp grassland, usually reach about 30-40cms, but the authors have found specimens as big as 75cm across, weighing 12kg. The white, football-like fruiting bodies reach their large size in only a few days usually in August/September and if picked whilst the spore filled area is still white and sliced into 2cm slices, can be fried like a piece of steak, the taste being similar. After a week or so the spores turn yellow and then later mid-brown. In dry weather the head then opens by a large pore on top and the spores are gradually shed into the wind. If detached from the hyphae the bodies turn dark brown and can persist for months. The Fairy-ring Toadstool, is frequently seen in short turf, the rings expand year by year, dying back behind the current growth. They are often associated with Neolithic sites, where legend has it that the fairies dwell, but can occur anywhere, even in lawns.

Look for Dead Man's Fingers, black, club-shaped, rough-surfaced and about 3-8cm high in the short grass on L'Ancresse Common in Guernsey and behind the sea wall in the middle of Longis Bay in Alderney. These are particularly noticeable in autumn and early winter.

Several species of Milk Cap, which exude a milky fluid when the fresh specimens are cut; (*Melanoleuca* spp.) and *Clitocybe,* the commonest of which is the Clouded Agaric, will also be found. It is best to consult a specialist book to separate them.

Less common are;

Common Morrel, usually about 7-10cm high, pear-shaped, like a yellow-brown net; Cauliflower Fungus, lives up to its name in appearance, is pale brown/white and can be 20-50cm across. Jew's-Ear, is gelatinous at first, drying to a thin hard, ear-shaped shiny brown excressence, about 5-8cm across, usually on branches of Elder. The Oyster Mushroom grows in large blue-grey/brownish clusters on Beech, Poplar and Willow. The gills are white, decurrent and the stem is off centre; Chanterelle, is found more rarely in deciduous woodland in late summer. The cap is depressed in the centre, tapering into the stipe, dark egg-coloured with decurrent pale yellow gills. Common Earthballs, (*Scleroderma* spp.), are usually found in short sandy turf, barely emerging from the ground in late summer to early winter. 5-7cm across, the fruiting body is rounded and creamy brown with large scales or darker with small brown scales, according to species. The flesh when cut has a thin creamy wall filled with dark brown spores.

On patches of horse dung or rotting straw bales, look for;

St. Aman's Cup, buff coloured cups lined with pinky orange, with inrolled margins, each about 5-8cm across in large clusters. In a similar situation you may find the Common Ink-cap and the Bell-shaped Mottlegill. This has 2-3cm pointed, bell-shaped buff caps, darker reddish-brown towards the centre on thin grey stalks 7-10cm high. The gills are black.

Rare, but especially noticeable when seen in roadside turf, is the Common Earth Star. The brownish globose 3-5cm head, stands up on the 4-8 pointed rays 6-10cm across, formed by the outer wall splitting and folding back and down like a saucer. The whitish inside revealed has a depressed pore in the centre through which the spores are shed. Even rarer, but found in Alderney on at least two occasions in the last few years, is the Perigord Truffle, greyish white about 5-7cm across, found almost buried under birch or beech trees in later summer as it comes to the surface.

There are many species of small fungi living on plants, in the soil and on decaying material some of which need the use of a microscope or at the very least a powerful hand lens to distinguish and identify them. The Dry-rot and Wet-rot fungi are very prevalent on the timber of old buildings in the islands but are not normally found 'in the wild'.

Amongst the larger of these micro-species, which are more readily identifiable, look for;

**In grassland** - Orange/yellow patches of *Clavulinopsis corniculata*, tufted dichotomously branched, about 3-6cm high; the Orange Peel Fungus, (*Aleuria aurantia*), forms patches of small bright orange cups, usually about 2-5cm across, with inrolled white margins, on bare patches in short grass from late summer to early winter. Look also on sandy calcareous grassland such as L'Ancresse, Longis and Herm Commons, for the pale ochre, globose head of *Tulostoma brumale*, 1-2cm across, on a 2-5cm slender stipe, tapering upwards. The spores are shed through a small circular pore on the top of the head, surrounded by a reddish brown cylindrical mouth. These commons are also a place to find the Scarlet Hood, the red pointed shiny caps, yellow towards the centre and later opening almost flat, are 2-4cm across on a 2-5cm stipe of the same colour. The gills are yellow at first and turn blood red with a yellow margin. Other *Hygrocybe* species also occur here.

**On decaying wood** - Velvet Shank, the small tan/yellow/orange mushroom, about 2-5cm across, with pale yellow gills, grows in clusters particularly on old elm stumps; *Dacrymyces stillatus* forms gelatinous orange/red cushions on dead branches of several trees and shrubs. It is particularly noticeable on old Gorse stems at any time of year. Silver-leaf Fungus, *(Chondrostereum purpureum)*, occurs on old stumps throughout the year. It forms a quantity of tough brackets about 3cm across and 3-5mm thick, bands of dense white woolly hairs alternate with darker brown or violet bands. Black Bulgar forms globose rubbery cups 2-4cm across. Black with a silvery sheen, they are tightly packed on old deciduous tree stumps and have inrolled margins. Usually found in autumn, but persisting through the winter.

## LICHENS

Lichens are formed by a symbiotic association of a fungus and an alga and are very susceptible to atmospheric pollution. The islands' unpolluted atmosphere, especially in Alderney, Sark and Herm, has helped to retain a number of species in this group which are generally declining in Britain.

Well over 300 species have been found in the islands and are perhaps best classified for identification purposes into their most likely habitats. Most do not have a common English name.

**SEASHORE**

Below HWM the wide spreading, black, tarry-looking, encrustation over many of the rocks is *Verrucaria maura*. Above this the bright orange patches are usually *Caloplaca marina*. Higher up the rock and cliff faces, the greenish white branched lichens are probably *Ramalina siliquosa* and the grey patches are *Lecanora* species, with *Parmelia* and *Umbilicaria* species on rocks in the splash zone and above.

On the intertidal rocks, dark-green patches of *Verrucaria mucosa* will sometimes be seen and blackish tufts of *Lichena pygmea*.
## TREES
The most common, flat, yellow or orange patches are often *Xanthoria parietina*, whilst clusters of *Parmelia, Usnea* and *Ramalina* species are also frequent epiphytes.
## WALLS
The orange-yellow patches on walls are often *Xanthoria aureola*, with *Parmelia* species frequent.
## SOIL
The most frequent lichens found growing on bare sandy ground and on the heath and moorland areas, are the yellow-green *Cladonia* species.
## CEMENT AND CONCRETE
These are usually first colonised by the black *Placynthium nigrum*, the yellow/orange *Coloplaca heppiana* and the brownish-green *Lecanora muralis*.

# THE BRYOPHYTES

The unpolluted atmosphere has enabled many species of the lower plants which have disappeared from the mainland to survive. Once again Marquand offers the most complete lists for Guernsey and Sark, with lists of lichens only from Herm, Jethou and Crevichon. His Alderney lists, and those of Rhodes in 1909, have been superseded by a comprehensive work on the Alderney Bryophytes by Dr. J.W. Bates, a member of the Department of Pure and Applied Biology at Imperial College, Silwood Park, Ascot, Berks, who wrote his manuscript as a result of visits to Alderney during April, in 1975, 1976 and 1988.

His full manuscript under the title **A BRYOPHYTE FLORA OF ALDERNEY,** was published in *Cryptogamie, Bryologie et Lichénologie* (1989, Vol 10 No.2) and an extract, (which gives the full list of Bryophytes recorded from Alderney to date), has been made by ourselves, with the full co-operation of the author. A copy of the original manuscript is held at the Alderney Society Museum and the extract was published in the Society's 1989 *Bulletin*.

The Alderney list now contains 30 species of liverworts and 138 species of mosses. Brecqhou has 6 liverworts and 21 mosses recorded.

### Mosses

Alderney has one speciality in this group, *Bartramia stricta*, a very rare moss in Britain where it is only known from one site in Wales, but quite plentiful in crevices in the cliffs between La Tchue and Hanging Rocks. It is its only known site in the Channel Islands.

It is not possible in a work of this nature to give comprehensive lists or assist the identification of the species found. The reader is referred to a specialist guide to enable them to identify the species they find in any of the islands.

In general however;

Hair Mosses, (*Polytrichum* species) and *Campylopus* species, are quite common on the moorland areas and some cliffs.

*Fissidens* species are common on grassy banks in dry, or moist shady, places, according to the species.

Catherine's Moss, (*Atrichum undulatum*) is quite common in woodland areas. The cushion-forming moss *Dicranum bonjeanii* is locally abundant, with *D. scoparium* common on some cliffs.

Three species of *Campylopus* are frequent along the cliffs, with *Ceratodon purpureus* and *Funaria hygrometica* very common in a number of places.

*Tortula ruraliformis* is abundant on sandhills, whilst *T. muralis* may be found on concrete, bricks and mortar, with *T. atrovirens* locally frequent and *Tortella flavovirens* abundant in the supralittoral zone.

Several *Hypnum* species will be found in marshy spots and on stones, trees, rocks and walls, with *Mnium* and *Dicranella* species also in the woods.

*Schistidium maritimum* is locally abundant on N. & E. facing cliffs. *Orthotrichum diaphanum* is common on concrete and is an epiphyte on walls and rocks.

*Drepanocladus aduncus* is abundant in and around some pools, whilst *Calliergonella cuspidata* is common in wet areas and is the dominant species in Berry's Quarry in Alderney.

## THE VASCULAR PLANTS

The reader is referred for the complete lists to the *Wild Flowers of Guernsey*, published in 1974 with a supplement in 1987, and to *Flora of Alderney, a Checklist with Notes* published in 1988, with an insert giving an updated species list and corrections noting current (changed) nomenclature, added in 1995. Wild Flowers of Guernsey is long out of print, but the Supplement, the Flora of Alderney and several small booklets or lists recently published about the floras of Guernsey, Sark, Herm, (see *Transactions* 1993) and Brecqhou (see *Transactions* 1988), are available from local book and paper shops and the Museums. More recent publications include a small volume; *Wild Flowers of the Bailiwick Of Guernsey,* illustrated with watercolours, published by La Société Guernesiaise and a *Field Companion; Flowers of Sark* by Ann Allen, illustrated with line drawings.

## 1. Lycopodiopsida.
The only families of this group of primitive plants represented are the Mossy Clubmoss in Fermain Valley, Guernsey and the rare Land Quillwort, known from L'Ancresse Common in Guernsey and four locations in Alderney, three near Fort Quesnard and one on Essex Hill.

## 2. Equisetopsida.
There are four species of Horsetail found in the islands, including the Great Horsetail. This is not particularly rare in Britain, but Alderney possesses the only Channel Island colony, in field edges and verges either side of the road, not far from the airport. Its fruiting stem, pale, almost colourless about 20cm high and 2cm across can usually be found March or April, long before the 1.5-2m vegetative stems appear. Water Horsetail is found only in a few swampy areas in Guernsey.

## 3. Pteropsida.
35-40 ferns have been recorded over the years, but most of them are rare or at least not very frequent. Royal Fern was an ancient inhabitant of Guernsey, whose spores have been found in the peat, but now only two specimens are known. A few planted specimens have survived for half a century or more in Alderney, Sark and Herm. A single patch of the rare Jersey Fern is known from Guernsey. Lanceolate Spleenwort is common in Guernsey, rare in Alderney and only occasional in Sark and Herm, whilst Rusty-back Fern is only known from a few small spots in Guernsey and Herm and three in Alderney. The Water Fern, (*Azolla filiculoides*) a subtropical species, may be found at the pumping station at King's Mills in Guernsey and in Corblets Quarry and Mannez pond in Alderney. It has been known in each location for many years but the quantity varies greatly from year to year. It also flourishes in several garden ponds.

Guernsey has its own specialities in the form of three natural hybrid ferns, the Guernsey Spleenwort, Jackson's Fern and the Guernsey Fern, the last two known for more than 140 years. Also in this category come the Small and Least Adder's-tongue Ferns already mentioned. Common Adder's-tongue however occurs in Guernsey, Alderney and Brecqhou.

Bracken is abundant throughout the islands, whilst Black Spleenwort, Hart's-tongue Fern, Male Fern, and Common Polypody are generally common. Classed as frequent in several of the islands are the Sea Spleenwort, Lady Fern, Golden-scaled Male Fern and Buckler Fern. Wall-rue is more frequently found in Alderney than in the other three islands.

Crevichon is comparatively rich in ferns, with six species found on its barely 3 acres.

**4. Pinopsida.** (Formerly known as Gymnosperms).

The present day members of this group have nearly all been planted. Most frequently encountered is the Monterey Pine. Much planted in the islands for its comparative resistance to salt winds, it has rarely, if ever, been known to seed itself in the wild. Many of the large specimens of the Monterey Cypress (up to 20m) formerly in Guernsey and Alderney were brought down in the 1987 hurricane or, in Alderney, have been removed since then, in the Banquage housing site clearance.

**5. Magnoliopsida.** (The group generally known as the "flowering plants", now divided into the Magnoliidae or Dicotyledons and the Liliidae or Monocotyledons).

It should be noted that many of the species noted in Marquand's *Flora* have not been found this century, whilst between 150-200 Guernsey species have been discovered since his time. Some 100 or more species have been added to the Alderney lists by post-war botanists, most of them by the present authors. Some of Marquand's records are now know by different names. Let us look briefly at some of the more unusual plants to be found today.

Visitors to the islands should be made aware that many plants, common in Britain, are absent or rare here. Some of the rarer plants there are quite common here, but others exist only in small, often isolated communities. A number of the species listed in the British Red Data Book are comparatively common in some parts of the islands.

The rarest of these was probably the Purple Spurge found in Alderney on shingle at Crabby and Saline Bays, almost certainly its last site in the British Isles and unfortunately now probably extinct. Botanists came from far and wide to see it, but after a great storm in the early 1970s greatly altered its shingle habitat, it has been sought in vain. It was last recorded from Jersey in 1928, Guernsey in 1931 and Herm in 1949 (and possibly again in 1968).

Alderney Sea Lavender, *Limonium normannicum* is unique to Alderney and Jersey. Closely related species are to be found on maritime rocks and dunes in a number of other places in the islands, as well as in the British Isles. It usually flowers in July and August in its one known site along the East coast. Of the other species, the most common is Rock Sea Lavender, (*L. binervosum*). This is widespread but not common along the cliffs in Guernsey, and in patches all around Fort Clonque in Alderney. Sark has its own variety, *L. binervosum* subsp. *sarniensis*, var. *serquense*.

The Alderney Geranium, *Geranium submolle*, is thought to be of South American origin and otherwise only exists in Guernsey. It has recently started to spread in Alderney, from the spot near Battery Quarry, where it was first found in 1938. Up to about 80cm high with its small pinky flowers borne in pairs, it flowers from May to September.

Bastard Toadflax has two small colonies at opposite ends of Alderney close to the shore and five others in different small areas on Longis Common. All the sites are shell rich dune areas. The number of plants at all seven sites has increased somewhat in recent years. It is also found in Jersey. In the British Isles this parasitic, lime-loving plant is otherwise only found in a few places on chalk grassland in England. The thin, olive-green prostrate stems bear many minute star-shaped, white 5-tepalled (not petalled) flowers, which may be found anytime between the end of May and October.

The Spotted Rock-rose is only otherwise to be found near the sea in W & SW Ireland, NW Wales and Jersey. In Alderney there is a fine area along the South Cliffs. This small annual drops its petals before noon, so must be looked for in the morning from June to August. Not far away from this on a rocky headland about 100ft above the waves, look for the Sea Purslane, a plant which normally grows at the edges of saltmarshes. In the Channel Islands it seems to prefer the cliff habitat and can be seen in a similar position above the Venus Pool in Sark and in odd spots along the south cliffs in Guernsey.

Our most common Fumitory, in all of the islands except Herm and Jethou, from which there is only one record each, is Boreau's Fumitory, *Fumaria muralis,* subsp. *boraei.* It is rarely found in Britain but here is in flower in most months of the year.

Flax-leaved St. John's-wort, *Hypericum linariifolium,* rare in England exists in two small areas in Guernsey and as a single small colony on a bare rock face below the South cliffs in Alderney.

Four-leaved Allseed, *Polycarpon tetraphyllum* is common in the Channel Islands, but usually only seen otherwise in Cornwall and the Scilly Isles. Look for it in bare sandy patches close to the sea, or as a garden weed in houses close to the sea.

Small Hare's-ear *Bupleurum baldense* grows in some quantity on the sandhills of Guernsey, at one spot on the east coast and on Longis Common in Alderney and very locally in Herm. This minute (2-3cm) plant of the parsley family (Umbelliferae) usually flowers in June. Another umbellifer, Alexanders, probably introduced by the Romans, is abundant in Guernsey and Herm, quite common in Sark but extremely rare in Alderney.

Of the leguminous plants, the Orange Bird's-foot, frequent on L'Ancresse Common and in Mannez Quarry and along the cliff paths in Alderney, grows only in the Channel and Scilly Islands; the Bithynian Vetch, rare and decreasing by the coast in Britain, may be found in several spots on the flatter parts of Guernsey and in one large patch at Crabby Bay, Alderney. Small Restharrow, rare in England

and Guernsey, absent from Jersey, still has a tenuous hold in one small patch on the east coast of Alderney where it had been known for more than 150 years. After being sought but not found by both local and visiting botanists for several years, in 1992, the authors noted about 100 plants in its original site. Similar numbers were found in 1993 and 1994. A tiny annual about 5-6cm high bearing pink and white flowers which are similar in size and appearance to the very common Restharrow, it usually flowers from May to June. In 1995 another colony of 50+ plants was noted on Mannez Hill at a spot which might well be the same as that recorded by Babington in 1838. Atlantic or Western Clover, *Trifolium occidentale,* is frequent round cliff edges and in short turf near the sea throughout the islands. Smaller than and flowering three to four weeks earlier than White Clover, *T. repens,* it has only been recognised as a separate species in the last decade or so. Black Medick, a common pest in lawns and pasture in Guernsey and Alderney is rare in Sark and Herm.

The parasitic Broomrapes are declining in the UK through the use of herbicides. Alderney is still blessed with a variety. The Purple Broomrape, *Orobanche purpurea,* growing on Yarrow is found frequently, even in lawns. It is absent from the other islands, except for two records in Guernsey, (1884 and 1992) and two in Sark in 1847 and 1977. The Greater Broomrape, *O. rapum-genistae,* makes a distinctive sight on the Prostrate Broom, *Cytisus scoparius* subsp. *maritimus,* on the Alderney's South cliffs, its only site in the Bailiwick, whilst the reddish, Carrot Broomrape *O. maritima,* is frequent along the seaward margins of the Alderney sand dunes but rare in the other islands. Common or Lesser Broomrape, *O. minor,* is just that in Alderney not very common in Guernsey and rare in Sark and Herm, but Ivy Broomrape, *O. hederae,* extremely common in Guernsey and frequent in Sark, has been found only along a single valley in Alderney, despite the vast quantities of Ivy everywhere. It is also rare in Herm. Broomrapes mostly flower in June and July, but their dried stems and flower cups often persist throughout the winter.

The variation between the islands is greater than the simple difference in total species numbers. That difference is most likely to be related to the more restricted number of habitats in the smaller islands which simply do not provide suitable conditions for many plants to grow. Wood Spurge for instance is absent from all of the smaller islands. The common Dog Violet of the islands is *Viola riviniana,* whilst *V. canina* is unknown. Guernsey also has the minute Dwarf Pansy, *V. kitaibeliana,* quite common on open sandy turf close to the sea, rare in Herm and unknown in Alderney, Sark and in Britain except for the Scilly Isles. The Great Sea Stock is rare in Guernsey and unknown elsewhere in the Bailiwick, whilst Sea Stock, known in Elizabethan times as "Garnesee Violets" was not recorded again until 1837 then vanished until 1934 and was found again in some of the northwest quarries in the 1950s, with both mauve and white flowers. Alderney has both colours in plenty, but the white-flowered form only occurs on the cliffs in Corblets Quarry, where the mauve variety is never seen. It is absent from Sark and Herm. Hoary Mustard, frequent on the dry sandy commons in Guernsey and Alderney is also absent from Sark and Herm. It is but recently found in England. Common Scurvy-grass seems to be confined to Alderney, whilst Danish Scurvy-grass is common throughout the islands.

The arable weeds are generally in great decline everywhere, differences in the islands are to a great extent reflected in the amount of land cultivated and the use of herbicides. Crops grown at various times in the past, particularly flower crops, also have a noticeable residual effect on the local flora, for instance; Guernsey airport was built, in 1937, on land where daffodils were formerly cultivated. In the spring hundreds may still be seen scattered in the grass surrounding the runway and taxiways. Ground Elder, a considerable pest on the mainland and in Jersey, especially in gardens, is fortunately rare throughout the Bailiwick and has only once been recorded in Alderney. Sharp-leaved Fluellen, widespread but not frequent in cornfields in Guernsey, present in some quantity in Sark, occasional in Herm, is virtually unknown in Alderney. On the other hand Black Bindweed, which has a similar habit and habitat, common in Alderney, is only occasionally found in the other islands.

Hound's-tongue is common in Herm, it is rare in Guernsey and unknown in the other islands. The tiny, red-leaved, Mossy Stonecrop, frequent in bare spots on cliff paths in Guernsey and Herm, common in Sark, is absent from Alderney. It flowers in April and May.

The St. Peter Port Daisy, *Erigeron karvinskianus*, a Mexican plant common on walls in Guernsey, especially round the town area, is also common in Jersey, has been seen occasionally in Sark, but is absent in the wild from the other islands. Cape Cudweed, *Gnaphalium undulatum*, is naturalised and frequent in all the Channel Islands but absent from Britain. About 80cm high, its strap-shaped leaves are bright green above and silvery white below, whilst Jersey Cudweed, *G. luteoalbum*, with furry white stems and leaves, up to 50cm high with tight heads of small yellow flowers is found very locally in Jersey, Guernsey, Alderney and W. Norfolk. Look for both in flower from June to September.

In three places in Alderney, most notably near the bottom of the Bonne Terre stream, at Platte Saline, in September and October the huge thistle-like heads of the perennial Globe Artichoke, *Cynara scolymus*, appear. These last are self-seeded from a crop grown in a nearby field in the 1950s. They have spread considerably in the last three or four years. Another huge thistle is the Cotton or Scotch Thistle, *Onopordum acanthium*, a biennial, well over six feet high when mature, with silver-grey foliage and comparatively small flower heads. It first appeared in Auderville in 1991, was noted in a meadow along the Longis Road in 1993 and on Braye Common in 1994 and 1995. Its flower is the emblem of Scotland, but it is rarely found there and was probably introduced to the British Isles in the 16th century. It was planted in the grounds of Fotheringay Castle, whilst Mary Queen of Scots was imprisoned there, which probably accounts for its use as the emblem. Its only Guernsey record is about 1788.

The Dwarf Rush, *Juncus capitatus,* first found in Guernsey in 1780, is quite frequent in the Vale and on the south cliffs in Guernsey and may be found in two small patches on the cliffs around the Giffoine in Alderney. It has also been reported from Sark and Herm. In the UK it exists only in W Cornwall, where it is very rare. It was formerly also found in Anglesey.

Wild Asparagus survives on the cliffs at Pleinmont but is unknown elsewhere in the islands. It is rare and decreasing round English and Welsh coasts. Autumn Squill, like a miniature Bluebell, is common in the sandy turf close to the sea throughout the islands, but more or less confined to SW England.

Several unusual members of the Lily family can be seen in the islands. Star-of-Bethlehem, *Ornithogallum umbellatum,* can be found in fields above Valongis in Alderney, probably as a remnant of a flower crop from the 1960s. A few specimens can also be found in wall tops and banks, notably near the Golf Club. The very similar appearing Guernsey Star-of-Bethlehem, *Allium neapolitanum,* is common in that island, but not elsewhere.

Spring Starflower, *Tristagma uniflorum,* thrives in a dry wall near Essex Castle in Alderney and, much more surprisingly grows out of the ashphalt roadway, along a wall bottom in Route des Mielles. Flowering in February, or even January in a mild winter, a native of South America, it is naturalised in West Cornwall, the Scillies and in small numbers in the Channel Islands. The Cuban Lily which, despite its name probably originates in the Mediterranean; the African Lily, the Jersey Lily, the Guernsey Lily, known there since about 1650, Summer Snowflake, and a species of Crinum, *C. powelli,* may all be found in their seasons in scattered localities. These are all probably garden escapes or may have been deliberately planted out "in the wild" at some time in the past, and have survived and multiplied. Ramsons or Wild Garlic, (*Allium ursinum*) common in England is unknown in the islands, its place being taken by the Three-cornered Leek, (*A. triquetum*), usually known throughout the Channel Islands as " Stinking Onions" a Mediterranean plant which is now widespread here.

The Sand Crocus, *Romulea columnae,* thrives along the cliffs and in the sandy north of Guernsey and Herm, on the cliffs near Essex and on the East coast at St. Esquerre in Alderney and in Sark. It is also found very locally in Devon.

Another member of the lily family, the New Zealand Cabbage Palm, *Cordyline australis* will be noted frequently, both in and out of gardens in all the islands. Those originally planted all along Braye Bay in the 1930s, were about 12-15 feet tall until the 1987 hurricane cut them back, but almost all have grown up again from the base. They flower regularly and set seeds quite frequently.

Less frequent outside gardens, but still noted in a few fields well away from houses, New Zealand Flax, is unmistakeable. Large rosettes of 1-3m long sword-like leaves give rise, in August and September, to dark brown stems up to 4m high and 5cm across, bearing towards the top a large number of strange looking brownish-red cigar-shaped flowers with an inner greeny-yellow ring.

Of the Arums, Lords and Ladies (*A. maculatum*) is common in Guernsey and frequent in Sark. It is not usually found in Alderney or Herm where the Large Lords and Ladies (*A. italicum*) thrive. This species is not common in Guernsey. Of the Duckweeds, Ivy-leaved Duckweed is abundant some years in Mannez pond, Alderney and unknown in the other islands. Alderney also has the only colonies of the Least Duckweed, found by the authors in 1992 and 1995. The Lesser Reedmace is known only from two or three places in Guernsey and one in Alderney.

The grass flora of the islands varies widely. Some strange grasses may be noticed, including Bermuda Grass, at Vazon and along other parts of the west coast of Guernsey and near the Targets at Longis in Alderney. About 10-15cm high, the flowering head has five brown rays of florets, arranged like the spokes of an umbrella in August and September. Dwarf Millet is another Guernsey speciality never found anywhere else in the British Isles. Early Sand-grass was first noted in Guernsey in 1787. Barely 5cm high its tiny clumps, flowering from January to May, are frequent along the cliffs and sandy coasts, there and in Herm. It seems to be absent from Alderney and Sark. In the UK it is only known from Anglesey. Sand Cat's-tail is common in Alderney and Herm, but not very frequent in Guernsey and absent from Sark. Hare's-tail Grass, common in the short turf of fixed dune areas in Guernsey and Jersey has only been reported on one or two occasions in the other islands.

Of the Quaking-grasses, Great Quaking-grass is naturalised in several places, usually close to the sea, in Guernsey and Alderney, Quaking-grass has been recorded in Alderney, whilst Lesser Quaking-grass is frequent in Guernsey, found along several roadsides in Sark, but absent from the other islands. Two species of Canary Grasses, *Phalaris minor* and *P. canariensis,* are scattered in the sandy areas of Guernsey and Alderney. A number of other bird-seed casuals are found, whilst the pretty little Yellow Bristle Grass, may be noticed near the Essex Manor restaurant in Alderney. One of the strangest named grasses in Alderney is the Rescue Brome, *Bromus wildenowii.* Found only in Barrackmaster's Lane near the Devereux House

Hotel, it is a very sturdy plant about 1.5m high, flowering from May to October. It is occasionally reported in Guernsey, is locally plentiful in Jersey, but is not recorded from Britain. Nit-grass, found along a number of roadsides in Sark, has only two records in Guernsey this century although it was once more widespread. It is unknown from the other islands.

There is a small pond on Lihou island which supports a number of saltmarsh plants, these include; Saltmarsh Rush, Prostrate Glasswort, Common Seablite and Sea Milkwort. The shingle bank on the island supports the plants commonly found in Guernsey in this habitat, and for one year only, in the late 1980s, Sea Pea, *Lathyrus japonicus* appeared.

Various pondweeds, including Stoneworts flourish in the 25+ small water-filled quarries in Guernsey. Of these 17 are in the Vale Parish.

Orchids are in fairly short supply throughout the islands, Autumn Lady's Tresses are frequent only in Guernsey and Alderney, although it is also present in Sark; the Green-winged Orchid only in Alderney; the Loose-flowered Orchid is confined to a small area of Guernsey, where it grows in some quantity and the Pyramidal Orchid is only in Alderney, where it is common on the dry sandy areas. Bee, Southern Marsh, Common Spotted and Heath Spotted Orchids are occasional in Guernsey and rare in Alderney. The Heath Spotted is also found in Sark beside two streams.

Sark has a number of flowers which are not commonly found in some of the other islands. Sea Plantain, locally frequent, is seen most easily just over the wall on the left as you come up the slope from the Masseline Harbour. It is also ' local' in Guernsey, where it seems to be increasing, but absent from Alderney and Herm. Hemp Agrimony, particularly attractive to butterflies, grows in some quantity beside the footpath up the Harbour Hill. Widespread but not plentiful in damp spots in Guernsey, this is not recorded from the other islands. Along the same path look for the huge, almost circular leaves up to about 80cm across, of Giant Butterbur, *Petasites japonicus,* found nowhere else in the Channel Islands. The ordinary Butterbur is not found at all in the Bailiwick. Yellow Pimpernel, found in several wet valleys, is also absent from the rest of the Bailiwick.

The Beach Strawberry, *Fragaria chiloensis,* (one of the parents of the Garden Strawberry), is also only found in Sark, growing for many years in some quantity on a bank in the Seigneurie Gardens. Unfortunately it is a dioecious plant and only the male plant is present. The Wild Teasel, an unexpectedly rare plant in the Channel Islands, grows above Grande Grève and Rouge Terrier. The Deptford Pink is another rare plant found here and in two spots in Guernsey.

A few of the Channel Island specialities were introduced to gardens and survive either there, or after escaping in the wild, because of the comparative lack of frost and snow. The most spectacular looking to most visitors is probably the Giant Echium, a close relative of the Viper's Bugloss. Originating on mountainsides in the Canary Islands, the mauve flower spikes can reach over 20ft in height. They appear to grow on a triennial cycle in the islands. The first year a flat rosette of leaves, about 30-40cm across, gives rise to a stem, about 1m high with leaves up to ½ m long in the second year. The usually single flower stem rockets up from this in the third season, flowers for many weeks and then dies leaving a gaunt blackened spike persisting through much of the winter. It seeds profusely and has escaped from gardens to the wild in many places. Other less obvious plants are the Hedge Fuchsia (*F. magellanica*) planted as a garden hedge in many places, but often noted on the cliffs and sandy land near the sea, which can reach 10-15 feet in time. It spreads by both seed and suckers and is more or less evergreen. Another tangled, arching, hedge-like plant, is the Duke of Argyll's Tea Tree. A member of the potato family from China, this bears small purplish flowers for much of the year. It suckers vigorously and is usually found close to the sea in Alderney. It was introduced from there to Guernsey about 1850. After severe salt winds it may loose its leaves but quickly grows new ones. Another sprawling potato family plant, this one from South America, Cock's-eggs, is found in several places in Guernsey, but not in the other islands.

Several other evergreen hedging plants which can resist salt winds are planted in the islands, especially near the sea and seed themselves regularly. Amongst these look for *Escallonia macrantha,* a member of the Gooseberry family, with dark green leaves and either deep red or pink flowers in bloom in most months of the year. *Eleaeagnus* species have waxy dark green leaves, with furry silver or glandular bronze backs depending on the species. Their small white trumpet shaped flowers appear in late autumn and are followed by red oval fruits. Most frequently grown as a dense hedge, left untended they reach 15-20 feet. The Japanese Spindle-tree is similar in growth habit and bears clusters of small green flowers in May. After a very warm summer these are followed by red, four-angled fruits. This is probably the most widely planted evergreen hedge in Alderney. A number of species of *Olearia* are grown for the same purpose, mostly in Guernsey. These are shrubby members of the Daisy family and their flowers vary from inconspicuous clusters of tiny heads like groundsel in *O. traversii,* to the large white clusters of the New Zealand Holly, (*O. macrodonta*). Hebe species, frequently the mauve Hedge Veronica (*H. x franciscana*), also make excellent hedging near the sea. They too are in flower for most of the year and seed freely around their bases. The 1987 hurricane killed most of the hedges of this species (as well as doing great damage to the others listed above) but they are now once again about 1.5m high, regenerated from the seedlings. They can be seen in many gardens and a few spots on the cliffs and growing on walls. Tamarisk has been planted in many places near the sea, especially by the Victorians. Its delicate pink flower heads appear several times in the year and many of the larger trees are well over 100 years old.

Guernsey is the home of, in the main, two types of Elm, the commonest, *Ulmus minor* or *U. sarniensis,* is known locally as the Male Elm from its upright habit with the side branches turning up parallel with the perfectly staight main trunk. The other, less common, is the distinctive Hybrid Guernsey Elm, *U. x hollandica,* known locally as the Female Elm. This has an irregular main trunk and spreading branches. These two lined almost every road and hedgebank until the Dutch Elm disease decimated the population. Despite magnificent attempts by the States of Guernsey, over many years, to fell and burn all affected trees as soon as the signs appeared, few are now left and the suckers which arise from them get affected as soon as they reach about 5-7cm in diameter. In Alderney and Herm they have been virtually wiped out, whilst Sark, despite the ravages of the disease, still retains some in the interior wooded valleys. Sark also has its own species, the White Elm, *U. laevis,* not known from any of the other islands. Wych Elms are rare and almost invariably planted.

With the demise of the Elm, the commonest tree in the islands today is probably the Sycamore, introduced in the Middle Ages and including many specimens with purple backs to their leaves. This tree self seeds to such an extent as to be a pest in the larger islands. The Field Maple however is unknown today, although its pollen occurs in the Vazon peat.

This brief list should help to give both residents and visitors a taste of the less common plants to be found in the islands.

An avenue of Guernsey Elms

*Chapter 6*

# MARINE ANIMALS

For descriptions and illustrations of the various vertebrate and invertebrate animals which come within this category, the reader is once again referred to one of the many specialist guide books to shore life which are available. This chapter simply gives a note of those species which may frequently be observed in most of the islands. The lists are by no means complete, no thorough survey having ever been carried out to the best of our knowledge. A few of the species, such as the Ormer, are at the northern limit of their range and will rarely if ever be found along the south coast of England.

## Invertebrates.

### 1. COLONIAL ANIMALS

Many of the animals in this group are so small as to form part of the free floating or swimming plankton and are only readily identified by using a microscope. However, a wide range of sponges, ascidians, sea squirts, hydroids, sea anemones and jellyfish etc. will be found on, or under, rocks; as epiphytes on various algae, especially the laminarians; or occasionally free-floating. The reader is again referred to the specialist guide books on this subject. Those most commonly seen are;

**Sponges;** White, orange, green, yellow, red or brown Breadcrumb Sponges, *Halichondria panicea,* in colonies usually less than 20cm across and up to 2cm thick. These encrust seaweeds, stones and rocks, especially on their underhanging surfaces from the middle shore down into deep water.

**Ascidians;**
**a. Sea Squirts;** several different types may be noted, solitary or in small groups. They are usually found near LWM or below, attached to rocks or large seaweeds. They have upright bodies with smooth swellings and two body openings, a 'mouth' at the top and an exhalant opening in the side about half way up. Pale, almost translucent and up to 10cm high is *Ascidia mentula;* brown; rougher looking and up to 6cm high is probably *Ascidiella aspersa*. Neither have common names. Look also for the almost transparent 'vases' up to 3cm of *Clavelina lepadiformis,* with the two siphons close together at the top and the spiral, orange, body contents showing through the tunic. More easily spotted and beautiful in a variety of colours are the;

**b. Star Ascidians;** although members of the same class, these are flat, colonial and the colonies are embedded in a transparent cellulose sheath. The colonies of 3-12 groups of individuals may all be yellow, brown, green or red star-shaped, each colony arranged in a circle or oval round a common exhalant cavity, *Botryllus schlosseri,* or with the groups either side of an elongated exhalation cavity and coloured orange, yellow or blue-grey, *Botrylloides leachi.* Look for them on smooth rock surfaces and some of the larger fucoids.

**Hydroids;** such as *Obelia* are generally almost transparent, have soft, sac-like bodies and live in flower-like colonies, attached at the base to rocks and seaweeds. They are amongst the commonest and most varied groups of marine animals but are usually overlooked. One of the generations in their life cycle is a minute free-swimming medusa, a jellyfish-like larva. The reader is again referred to specialist books for their identification.

**Jellyfish;** of the free-floating or swimming jellyfish, all of which can sting, The Portuguese Man-of-War has a body 30 x 10cm, silver, blue and red with, attached to it, large numbers of very long mauve/blue tentacles with a dangerous sting. It has been seen floating on occasions in several bays. The Octopus Jellyfish up to 60cm across and massive, whose sting does not usually trouble humans and the Compass Jellyfish which does, are sometimes found washed up, particularly after a violent storm at sea in the summer. The Common Jellyfish, almost transparent white, with four conspicuous purply, horse-shoe shaped reproductive organs (when seen from above), is sometimes seen swimming in groups close inshore in the summer and autumn. Although it can grow up to 25cm across, those most frequently seen are rarely more than about 10cm. Its sting is not usually troublesome to humans.

The 5-10cm high, pink/red, Stalked Jellyfish, is found attached to seaweeds in pools or on the lower shore. It is trumpet-shaped and has eight clusters of red tentacles arranged round the open end.

**Sea Anemones;** of the many types of Sea Anemone to be found, those most commonly seen are; the Beadlet Anemone, *Actinia equina,* in red, strawberry and green forms, up to about 7cm, but usually nearer 3-4cm. It retracts into an almost closed ball as the tide recedes and is able to stand several hours exposure at each tide. It is very common on rocks in the middle shore, whilst the larger 10-12cm Snakelocks Anemone, in both green and grey forms cannot retract its tentacles and is only to be found in permanent pools or from just below LWM down to about 20m.

The Trumpet Anemone, *Aiptasia couchi,* at a maximum of about 6cm high, has up to 80 tapering golden-brown tentacles, whilst the slightly smaller but not too different-looking *Anthopleura thallia,* has about 60 translucent ones.

**Corals;** Several kinds of the beautiful little so-called Jewel Anemones, *Corynactis viridis,* can be found, but these are actually true Corals. Their tentacles are arrranged in three circles and have coloured blobs on the ends. Soft Corals also occur, the one most likely to be encountered, under overhanging rocks in deeper water at very low tides, is Dead Man's Fingers, the colonies often looking rather like a ghostly white or pale yellow glove. The many individual polyps give it a rough appearance with their retractable tentacles, up to 1cm long.

**Sea Mats,** of various species, most commonly *Membranipora membranacea,* are frequently found encrusting the larger algae from the middle shore zone down to just below LWM. These will be particularly noted on the larger algae in patches of driftweed washed up by the tide, looking like a covering of white snakeskin.

## 2. VARIOUS WORMS

A rare flatworm, *Convoluta roscoffensis* may be found in the fine gravel at Clonque in Alderney. Small (0.5-1cm) like a lanceolate leaf, its green colour is due to a symbiotic single-celled green alga. Walking on the gravel nearby causes them to disappear below the surface. Two other rare worms *Balanoglossus sarniensis,* up to 30cm long, and *Golfingia vulgare,* live around the Vermerette Rock in Herm. Another marine worm *Loimia medusae* was found in some quantity on Herm Beach in 1978.

The Sea Mouse is a large scaly worm 10-20cm, its oval body is covered in green/grey/brown hairs along it dorsal surface. It prefers to live in a soft substrate in shallow water.

The commonly found segmented worms, several of them dug for on the sandy beaches and used as bait, are Lugworm, up to 20cm., browny-green with reddish gills on the hind 2/3rds, Ragworm, up to 12cm., green, pink and yellow and Paddleworm, 15-30cm, mauve and yellow-green. Catworms, grey to brown up to about 25cm. long are also found in the same areas.

A bristle worm, the Green Leaf Worm, 5-15cm. with up to 200 segments has a vivid green colour. It lives in rock crevices on the lower shore. Free swimming, it lives on barnacles. In the spring look for its eggs, small green spots in little bags of translucent jelly. The long (30-60cm) Rock Worm, brown with reddish gills on the lower 2/3rds and a green stripe along its back also lives in rock crevices on the lower shore.

The Sand Mason is up to 30cm long and covers itself with a single layer of sand grains. Much of it remains buried with only the several tentacles above the sand level. These often remain above the sand on the middle shore at low water and show as clusters of sandy threads. The Fan or Peacock Worm, grows up to

25cm and is also found on the middle shore. It has a membraneous, free-standing tube, the ring of gills around the top forming a retractable crown. Both are common and will be found in most sandy bays.

Other Tubeworms found, which form a calcareous shell attached to rocks or on fronds of Laminaria and Fucus, are usually species of one of the following. *Spirorbis*, (the most common), the abundant small white shells of *S. spirorbis*, which are coiled almost into a circle on the seaweeds, or the ridged, only slightly curved shells of *S. tridentatus*, found on rocks. *Pomatoceros triqueter*, which is triangular in section, and variable in colour, is found under stones or on dead shells on the lower shore or in shallow water. *Hydroides norvegica*, the twisted and interlaced, 3cm., brownish-white shells of which may be seen also on stones and shells. These are all attached to the substrate all along their length. *Serpula vermicularis* is attached only at the base, it exhibits circular growth rings up its shell and is found on rocks and old shells at the bottom of the tide. The tube of this last is pinky or greenish-brown with red gills, trumpet shaped, tapering to a point at the base and about 5-8cm long.

## 3. STARFISH & SEA URCHINS

Large starfish are not commonly found alive in the littoral zone, but small specimens of the Common Starfish occur. The more usual and quite common species seen is the green Cushion Star. The Goose-foot Star, whitish, with the margin and five divisions on top of the shell marked out in red, is occasional and various Brittle-stars are quite frequent. The many colour varieties of *Opiothrix fragilis*, often red and white or yellow, will be found under stones and seaweeds on the lower shore. *Amphipholis squamata*, smaller and grey/blue/white uses the same habitats, but is especially found amongst Corallina. The red-brown Feather Star may be found under rock overhangs or in crevices in rock pools and on the lower shore.

The Green Sea Urchin, grows to about 3-4cm and is found on and under stones, on the lower shore. The dark purple Rock Urchin, is about the same size, but generally lives in groups in hollows it has ground out of the rocks. Small specimens of the pinky red with white spines, Edible or Common Sea Urchin, which grows to about 10-12cm. may be found in this zone, but larger specimens are usually only found offshore. It grazes on rocks and Laminarians. Sand coloured Sea Potatoes, 6-9cm. across are quite common in the lower intertidal zone, burrowing into the sand and leaving a hole to mark their presence.

In this same class are the Sea Cucumbers; the Cotton Spinner, at about 20cm is the largest. Black/brown above and green/yellow below, it moves slowly on three rows of suckered tube-feet, usually amongst Zostera from the lowest shore level down to about 70m. Much smaller (4cm), and pinky coloured, the Sea Cucumber, is occasionally found.

## 4. CRUSTACEA

On the upper shore look out for;

Various Sand-hoppers amongst stones and rotting seaweed. Often present in large numbers, on a warm day the bites of these can be troublesome. The two most common species are *Talitrus saltator,* about 2.5cm., on the upper shore amongst the weed, with *Orchestria gammarella,* slightly longer and slimmer, amongst rocks and weed lower down the beach.

The Sea Slater, at 2.5cm long, looking like a large woodlouse with two forked tails will frequently be found on larger rocks at the top of the tidal zone. Usually hiding in crevices during the day, it moves very rapidly over the rocks in the evening. Be careful to distinguish these from the smaller Bristle-tail, which has three single bristles at its tail end, the longer central one equal to the body length. This animal is actually an insect, not a crustacean.

On rocks, exposed at some state of the tide;

The Barnacle *Chthamalus stellatus,* is generally found in the splash zone, often forming a complete encrustation across some rocks, as does the Acorn Barnacle, *Semibalanus balanoides,* a little further down the shore in the intertidal zone, differing from the other barnacle in the slightly different arrangement of its five shell plates. The first is almost at the northern limit of its range and is not found in the eastern English Channel or the North Sea, whilst the second species is nearly at the southern limit of its range and does not occur in the Bay of Biscay.

Look particularly for the Darwin Barnacle, *Elminius modestus,* on rocks in the upper or middle shore. This Australian barnacle is similar in appearance to the above, but only has four plates to its shell. It was first noted near Southampton during the last war and has spread rapidly along the Channel into the Atlantic. It has been found in Guernsey on several occasions now, and was first reported from Alderney in 1977. All three of the above are about 1-1.5cm in diameter.

Further down the shore, two larger barnacles 2-3cm may be noticed, both with six plates. The larger, *Balanus perforatus* occurs first. Its purplish cone has a serrated opening, slightly off centre, making it look like a volcano. Lower down the shore, the slightly smaller *B. crenatus,* is pale grey-brown and found at the bottom of rocks, just where they meet the sand. The plates on one side are longer than those on the other, making this one appear to be toppling over.

Occasionally large pieces of driftwood will be found encrusted with the Goose Barnacle, *Lepas anatifera.* This large barnacle the shell of which grows to about 5cm, has a 10-20cm long grey or brown stalk, the skin of which is somewhat retractable, shortening it considerably. The 5 plates of the shell are translucent white with bluish/orange edges. The whole animal hangs down underneath the floating timber or from the bottom of boats. In Elizabethan times it was still thought to be a plant and that the shells were the eggs from which Barnacle Geese hatched. A long entry is included in Gerarde's *Herbal or History of Plants,* published in 1597. This idea was mentioned by Theophrastus as far as back as 350BC.

In tidal pools at varying levels of the beach, usually under stones, or on weed, look for;

Prawns; commonly the almost transparent *Palaemon serratus* and the smaller Chamaeleon Prawn, *Palaemonetes varians,* may be found. This may be brilliant green, brown, or a variety of mottled colours taken from the habitat of the moment. The Common or Sand Shrimp, buries itself in the sand and can assume a similar colour to the particular substrate, making it difficult to find. If exposed in daylight it quickly covers itself by sweeping out a depression with its legs and then fanning the sand back over its body. It can be collected by pushing a shrimp net along the surface of the sand in shallow water. The Ghost Shrimp, is frequent in shallow pools and almost transparent, only its black eyes showing clearly.

Crabs; the Chancre or Edible Crab and the Spider Crab, both species are caught and eaten locally, small specimens will often be seen in the permanent pools. Fiddler or Velvet Swimming Crabs, also known locally as Lady Crabs are also eaten and all three species are sold in the Guernsey fish market. The Shore Crab, Porcelain Crabs, usually *Porcellana platycheles,* the Hairy Crab, and several Hermit Crabs, most commonly *Eupagurus bernhardus,* can also be found. These last take over the empty shells of a number of molluscs, changing to a larger one as they grow. They will often be seen running across the bottom of a pool or the wet sand, as the tide recedes.

Lobsters; the Squat Lobster, rarely more than 5cm across, will often be found under stones in the tidal zone in the spring when it migrates inshore and small specimens, up to 5cm of the smooth, brownish-blue coloured Edible Lobster, may also be seen on rarer occasions. Larger specimens might be found in deep pools in the summer. Less frequent are small specimens of the Crayfish, generally brown or purplish with pale spines on the shell, it is easily distinguished from the Lobster by the long, whip-like antennae and the lack of the large pincers on the first pair of walking legs.

## 5. MOLLUSCS

A wide range of molluscs will be encountered at various levels on the shore, the commoner of which, starting from the top of the beach, are;

Giant Horsetail cone            Bastard Toadflax. (Flowers 2mm across)

Bird's-foot (Fls. 3mm)

Orange Bird's-foot

Small Hare's-ear (15mm)

Annual Rock-rose

Alderney Sea-lavender. A very rare plant

Land Quillwort, a pteridophyte

Marsh Pennywort

Small Restharrow. An endangered species

Slender Bird's-foot-trefoil

Golden Samphire

"Guernsey Star-of-Bethlehem" (Neapolitan Garlic)

Flax-leaved St. John's-wort. Another rare plant

Least Adder's-tongue
A special Guernsey Fern

Rustyback Fern
Rare in the Bailiwick

Giant Butterbur. A Sark rarity

Pencilled Crane's-bill, another uncommon plant

Lampranthus is often seen on the cliffs

Bluebells on Burhou

Cotton Thistle on Braye Common   Lady's Bedstraw growing in a wall

Sand Crocus on the cliffs   Burnet Rose on Herm Common

Prostrate Broom and Thrift on the cliffs

Pyramidal Orchid

Green-winged Orchid

Bee Orchid

Autumn Lady's-tresses

Bermuda Grass

91

Young Shags on Longue Pierre off Herm

Shag's nest on Galeu

Loose-flowered Orchid. A Guernsey speciality

Lesser Black-backed Gull nest on Longue Pierre

Les Amfroques (The Humps) from Herm

Guernsey Cattle in Spring Meadow, Herm

Milking on Chouet Headland, Guernsey, 1985

Horticulture in the Vale, Guernsey

Gannets nesting on Les Etacs, Alderney

Sunset over the Hanois Lighthouse, Guernsey

Sunset over Fort Clonque, Alderney

Sunset from Herm Harbour

(a.) In the splash zone, an area not widely found on the more accessible parts of Alderney and Sark shores, is the tiny (5mm), smooth, blue-black, Small Periwinkle, *Littorina neritoides*. Able to withstand long periods of desiccation it hides in the small crevices in the rocks.

(b.) Through most of the intertidal range the Rough Periwinkles, *L. saxatilis* and *L. rudis* may be found in a variety of dull colours, on and under rocks, as may be Chitons, very primitive creatures found as huge fossils in some parts of the world. Ours are generally about 1-1.5cm long, either the brown, *Lepidopleurus asellus* or the more common, green *Lepidochitona cinereus*. Able to cling closely to rock surfaces, they graze across the surface of rocks and seaweeds, whilst the smooth Round or Flat Periwinkle, *L. littoralis,* bright yellow, orange or red-brown grazes mainly on fucoids in the same range. The 2cm. Edible Winkle, *L. littorea* is quite rare in Alderney and apparently absent from Sark and Herm, its place being taken in local diets by the common Toothed Winkle or Thick Topshell, *Monodonta lineata,* also 2cm., found in considerable numbers, mostly in the mid-tide range.

Three species of Topshells, *Gibbula* spp, Grey, (*G. cineraria*), Purple, (*G. umbilicalis*) and Large, *G. pennanti,* (which is not found on the English side of the Channel), are common in the middle-lower zone, and several species of Needle and Spire shells. The Purple or Flat Topshell, can easily be distinguished by the small hole or umbilicus on its lower surface. The beautiful Painted Topshell, up to 2.5cm high and about as broad, will be found at the bottom of the tide, under seaweeds and overhanging rocks.

Large, Common Limpets, *Patella vulgata,* greenish blue or grey with a rounded outline, up to 7cm across, abound throughout the range on rocks. The comparative height/width ratio of their shells varies markedly according to the direction of exposure to wave motion. The more sheltered specimens tend to be much taller than those on exposed surfaces. About the same size with a more orange top to the shell and short, darker rays around the irregular base is, *P. aspera*. This species, near the northern limit of its range here, tends to live in pools in the the lower shore zone. The smaller Limpet, *P. intermedia* (*P. depressa*), about 4cm and darker than the other two, may be found on exposed rocks in the middle tide range. In prehistoric times limpets must have formed a considerable part of the diet of people living in the islands, large quantities of their shells having been found in most of the Neolithic burial chambers. In the same area, the Keyhole Limpet, *Diodora apertura,* has a greyish-white, 4cm, ribbed shell with an aperture at the top. The Blue-rayed Limpet, *Patina pellucida,* smooth, oval and about 1.5cm long, will be found on Laminaria at extreme low-tide.

Two types of Cowries, of which the European Cowrie, *Trivia monacha,* is much the more common will be seen crawling about on the rocks and seaweeds on the lower shore. They feed on the various colonial Ascidia which grow attached to the rocks and larger algae in this area. Look for the round, white, Chinaman's Cap, 3-5cm across, the occasional Sting Winkle or Oyster Drill, *Ocenebra erinacea,* and the closely related *O. aciculata* with brilliant red flesh. This species is at the northern limit of its range and does not occur in England.

More commonly Dog-whelks, and the rarer Netted Dog-whelks, will be found. Dog-whelks are good indicators of sea pollution and are particularly sensitive to the TBT anti-fouling paint used on boats. This caused a considerable decline in their population a few years ago, particularly in harbour areas, but they are now recovering since the use of the chemical was prohibited. Unlike in Guernsey, they are not now very common anywhere in Alderney, even on shores well away from any anchorage. In surveys carried out by the authors in 1992 and 1993 for the Marine Conservation Society, few were found at any of eight sites, except in Clonque Bay. This seems to be a variation from the situation in 1970 when a Bailiwick survey was carried out and published in *Transactions,* (Brehaut, Vol XIX, Pt. 1, pp39-69), when numbers were similar. Large shells of the Whelk, *Buccinum undatum,* 9-10cm, are found washed up from time to time from deeper water, but they are rarely, if ever, seen alive.

Several types of Sea-slug may be found, some are pinky-coloured animals whose shells are often covered by their mantles; the brown Sea Hare, is a member of the same order, but with four 'horns' on its head, which grazes on seaweeds in shallow water and may discharge a purple dye if disturbed.

The yellow, warty, two-horned, Sea Lemon is about 7.5cm long. If you find it without disturbing it, (it too discharges a dye), you may well see the ring of nine retractable plumed gills around the anus. It feeds on the Breadcrumb Sponges. The Common Grey Sea-slug, up to 9cm, with four horns and many hornlike appendages in two rows down its back, feeds on the Snakelocks Anemone. Both are members of the order Nudibranchia.

Others, possibly small Squid, although these are seldom found close to the shore, and the shells of Elephant's Tusk, Razor Shells, (which bury themselves in the sand) and Cuttlefish 'bones' are frequently found, washed up on the beach. They are rarely seen alive, but are sometimes caught by local fishermen.

(c.) Sub-littoral zone; the largest mollusc of our shores, the Ormer, *Haliotis tuberculata,* which grows to about 10cm, once abundant, sadly has declined considerably in recent years and is most likely to be found below the lowest tide mark. It browses on red algae, principally Dulse, and rests under rocks and stones to which it attaches itself very firmly. It is now being farmed in Guernsey and shore gatherers in the islands also had better catches in 1993 and 1994. The gathering of Ormers is strictly controlled in the Channel Islands. They can only be gathered from the shore at certain of the lowest spring tides, the dates of which are advertised in the local papers and on radio and TV. Only those larger than a certain size can be collected and diving for them is prohibited. Gatherers usually use a special hook to enable them to detach them from their very firm hold on the rocks.

The Common Octopus, common around Alderney until about 1960 is now rarely found. Both of these animals are at the northern limit of their range and a slight drop in sea temperatures may be one of the reasons for their decline. Overfishing has also contributed.

Bivalves are not common on Alderney shores. Very small Scallops, Portuguese Oysters, and Dog Cockles are found. Common Mussels are also not frequent. They are occasionally found on rocks in Clonque, Longis, Platte Saline and Corblets Bays, and on the large driftwood timbers which support colonies of Goose Barnacles. A few Edible Oysters, *Ostrea edulis,* or perhaps the American, *Crassostrea virginica,* survivors of an Oyster-farming enterprise there in the 1960-70's, may be found in Longis Bay, but usually only as empty shells.

(d.) In deeper water, mature specimens of the European Oyster, Scallops and Mussels may be found in certain areas round the coasts and Guernsey fishermen bring in good catches. Like the Ormer, Scallops are subject to a minimum size restriction in order to conserve stocks. Large Dog Cockles are sold locally in restaurants as 'Clams', whilst Herm Oysters are famous throughout the islands.

The above lists are by no mean exhaustive. The diligent searcher in pools and under or on the rocks in the intertidal zone will doubtless discover many other species of invertebrate animals not recorded here. The authors would be pleased to learn of any such finds.

## Vertebrates.

### 6. FISH

A range of the fish caught by small boats at sea within a few hundred yards from the shore, or by rod and line from the shore or breakwaters is listed here, with only their common English names. The frequency with which the different species are caught is not indicated. Most are offered for sale in the Guernsey Fish Market. Alderney holds the British records for a number of species caught, usually in the annual fishing competitions, organised and sponsored by Aurigny Airlines. Fry of many of these species occur in the intertidal zone and are likely to be found in rockpools, frequently underneath rocks. These are included in the next section. Basking Sharks are occasionally seen all round the islands and rarely, even in Alderney Harbour.

From a list of the Guernsey dialect names of Insects, Birds and Fish published by E.D. Marquand in *Transactions* in 1908 (p. 512) one may safely assume that these are the species commonly caught in that island since much earlier times. The species mentioned in this list are underlined in the list which follows and varies little from those caught today.

Huss, Dogfish, Tope, Thornback Ray, Blond Ray, Sting Ray, Skate, Sprat, Herring, Garfish, Conger Eel, Cod (generally only up to 2kg), Pouting, Whiting, Pollack, Saithe, Ling, Rockling, Scad, Mackerel, Red Mullet, Bass, Sea Bream, Ballan Wrasse, Cuckoo Wrasse, Weever, Red Gurnard, Sandeels, Grey Mullet, Turbot, Brill, Plaice, Dover Sole, Cornish Sucker, Eel, Bullhead, John Doree, Topknot, Salmon, Monk Fish, Sand Smelt.

## LITTORAL ZONE FISH

Likely to be found in upper tidal pools;
Small specimens of Sole occur frequently, less frequently, Dab and occasionally Plaice fry may be seen in sandy pools;
Rock Gobies may be found in shallow pools, often under rocks and Sand Gobies live in pools with a sandy bottom. Gobies are collectively known in the local patois as *cabou*.
Usually in mid-tide pools;
Montague's Blenny, up to 8cm. brown with pale blue spots; Shanny, 10-15cm. yellow-brown to green with dark green spots, lives on the lower shore and in shallow water.
Tiny fry, up to 2-3cm, of the Thick-lipped Grey Mullet may be seen in large numbers in many pools. As they get bigger they swim in and out with the tide and larger specimens sometimes come inshore to feed, or adults in shoals to mate.
Small specimens of Sand-eels, both the Lesser and Greater, may be seen in rock pools, generally silvery coloured, the Greater is greenish along its dorsal side and has a black spot on the snout. They are sometimes found buried in the sand as the tide goes down and occasionally a thick line of dead ones can be found at the water's edge. Adults are about 20 and 30cm long respectively, they are much used for bait and are also the favourite food of the Puffin. In recent years a considerable decline in numbers may be due to over-fishing, a drop in water temperature, or both, and has probably contributed to the great reduction in Puffin numbers breeding on Burhou.
Three species of the interesting worm-like Pipefish may be found. They have ringed bodies, no ventral fins and usually only a small dorsal fin. The male carries the fertilised eggs in a pouch on his body after the female has placed them there.

The Worm Pipefish, about 15cm. long, are dark and frequent in tidal pools with plenty of weed cover. Clonque and Longis Bays are good places to find this species. The Lesser Pipefish, browner, but about the same length is generally found in shallow water. Around the entrance to the Inner Harbour in Alderney is one good spot. The much larger (up to 50cm.) Greater Pipefish may be found in the same area.

Montague's Seasnail, smooth, brown, about 7cm., with a rounded head and tapering body has a long dorsal fin and its two pelvic fins are modified to form a sucker. Look for it under stones in the pools in this part of the shore.

Usually at the bottom of the tidal range;

The Tompot Blenny may grow to as much as 25cm. and lives amongst stones and kelps. The Butterfly Blenny has a brown, spotted body about 15cm with large greenish fins. The first ray of the dorsal fin is about twice the height of the remainder and there is a large dark spot about half way along the fin. There are also two branched appendages above the eyes. Butterfish, a long thin fish up to 20cm, brown with a conspicous row of 11 dark spots along the base of its dorsal fin; Garfish, 30-80cm long, green and silvery white with a long jaw, forked tail and green bones lives in shoals near the surface and sometimes comes inshore. It is sold and eaten locally, but has a somewhat earthy flavour.

2-spotted Gobies, growing up to 6cm., live amongst Laminaria and lay their eggs on the holdfasts. Light brown in colour, their two conspicuous dark spots are just below the first dorsal fin and at the base of the tail. The Sand Goby grows to about 8-9cm, brownish, it has four darker vertical bands down its sides.

Sand Smelt, about 15cm. long, green above, silver below with a forked tail, sometimes swim in small shoals on the incoming tide. The Fifteen-spined Stickleback, the only marine Stickleback may be seen down to about 10m.

Lump Suckers or Sea Hens, a large rounded grey-blue fish up to 50cm, with four rows of conspicuous white bony knobs along the body are sometimes washed up. In the breeding season the lower half of the adult male turns bright pink. At the same time the upper half becomes much brighter blue, making it a very handsome fish. The Cornish Sucker, about 7cm. long, has a reddish flattened body with the dorsal and ventral fins joined to the tail. On top of its head behind the eyes are two large dark blue spots with a whitish ring round them. It clings to rocks in the lower tidal pools. Both have the pelvic fins modified to form a sucker. Other small sucker fish have been recorded from time to time.

The Lesser Weever, (beware !, it buries itself in the sand and, if trodden on can inflict painful, poisonous wounds from the spines on its gill covers and first dorsal fin). Small (12cm.), golden brown with many darker spots in rows along their length, these are sometimes reported from sandy bays.

Young Wrasse are also common in rock pools. Bright green young of the Ballan Wrasse are also found in the harbours. Several other brightly coloured species of Wrasse have been recorded.

Young Pollack are frequent in pools and many large specimens are caught in nets across Longis Bay just above low water, or with rod and line, all round the coasts. Up to 1.2m long these can weigh up to 3 kg.

Shoals of small specimens of Shore Rockling, dark purply-brown with three barbels on the head, 15-20cm when grown and the Five-bearded Rockling, brownish above greeny-silver below with five barbels and reaching 20cm when adult, occasionally swim in.

# 7. AQUATIC MAMMALS

## THE GREY SEAL

Seen on several occasions in most years, around our coasts, more frequently round Guernsey and on the reefs beyond Burhou, the seal has not been known to breed here, although young have been seen with their parents.

## DOLPHINS

Common Dolphin, Bottlenosed Dolphin and Porpoise are commonly seen round the coasts of Guernsey. Only rarely seen from Alderney as a passing shoal, a small group sometimes stays around the island for a few days and individuals of both Dolphin species have been recorded washed-up on the beaches, usually dead or injured. Off Alderney, a school of Porpoise is sometimes noted, either in the Race or the Swinge. Marquand included Porpoise in his 1908 list of patois names of "Fish" caught round Guernsey, noting that 'it was of course a mammal, not a fish'.

## WHALES

At various times a number of species of Whale have been seen swimming off the coasts, usually by local fishermen or from ferry boats.

In Guernsey in the last 75 years, the carcasses of about half a dozen whales have been washed up, including Pilot, Fin and Killer Whales. In Alderney in the same period, about a dozen specimens of different whales, including five Sei; a Sowerby's; a Pilot; a Killer; and a White Whale (on Platte Saline in January 1980); have been washed ashore and found dead or dying on the beaches. A magnificent effort by the Fire Brigade and many local residents on a hot summer's day, saved an 18ft. Minke Whale stranded on Bibette Head on 8th June 1982 (this was first identified as a Sei Whale). It was kept wet for several hours until the tide rose sufficiently to refloat it, when it was towed out to sea by Rowland Neal in his boat and, when released swam off, apparently unharmed.

*Chapter 7*

# FRESHWATER ANIMALS

## Invertebrates.

### 1. SINGLE-CELLED AND COLONIAL ANIMALS

Members of the sub-kingdom Protozoa; such as *Euglena, Amoeba* and *Paramecium* will only normally be seen under a microscope or with a powerful hand lens.

The sub-kingdom Parazoa is represented by the freshwater Sponges. The Pond Sponge forming greenish, branched, finger-like growths up to about 5-8cm. The sponge itself is creamy-white and owes its green colour to the presence of the alga *Chlorella*. It is usually attached to stones or submerged vegetation.

The River Sponge may be found encrusting stones, submerged roots or vegetation. It forms a soft flattish creamy-white mass, reaching about 2cm across. Amongst other places look for it on plant stems in the margins of ponds. In the autumn both species may be noted with spherical, brown, reproductive bodies studding their surface.

The sub-kingdom Mesozoa or multicellular animals includes all other animals, divided into their many classes.

The simplest colonial member is *Hydra* of which there are three species, look mainly for the Green Hydra about 5-10mm growing on the stems and leaves of other aquatic plants. The green colour makes it difficult to spot on the green host. *Rotifers* require a good microscope to enable you to see them at all.

### 2. VARIOUS WORMS

**Flatworms** (Platyhelminthes). Those most likely to be encountered are all species of planarians, found most commonly on the undersurface of stones and leaves on the bottom of ponds or crawling over the mud. They are generally less than 2cm long. They may be black, dark grey, brown, greenish or white. They feed on small animals, fish eggs etc. There are other smaller parasitic species.

**Roundworms** (Nematodes). These are threadlike creatures. Some are free living, but many are parasitic on or inside other animals.

**Hairworms** (*Gordius* species). The larvae are parasitic on water beetles, dragonflies etc, but the adults are common in ponds in early spring and summer. They resemble a horse hair about 10-15cm long.

**Segmented Worms.** A group which includes both segmented worms and leeches. The worms are generally found in the mud of pond and stream beds and are unlikely to be seen by the casual observer. The commonest leech is the Horse Leech, found in still waters and reaching 5-6cm. This is not a blood sucker, but swallows small worms, snails etc. It is very common in garden ponds.

## 3. CRUSTACEA

The **Water Louse** is quite common in ponds, springs and slow moving streams amongst the weeds. It is black and looks like a bristly Woodlouse, with two long feelers. Freshwater Shrimps are common and often appear in water emerging from land drains. They are a species of *Gammarus,* pinky-white and usually up to 2cm. Both species are scavengers, feeding on decaying plant and animal remains.

## 4. INSECTS

Insects which spend the greater part of their lives in or on water will be dealt with here, but it should be noted that the larvae of many flying insects are to be found in freshwater, especially in stagnant pools, ditches, rainwater barrels etc. Especially common are the red, wriggling *Chironomus,* (Midge) larvae. The pupae and larvae of Gnat and Mosquito will be seen close to the surface with their breathing tubes penetrating the water surface to reach the air and various dragonfly, may fly, caddis and many other fly nymphs may be seen in the water. These will be dealt with in Chapter 10 with the other insects.

**Water Bugs,** Hemiptera, all of which can fly, are represented most commonly by the Water Boatman, about 2cm. long which swims underwater. It chirps like a cricket if lifted out onto dry land; the larger Backswimmer, with longer legs and a keeled thorax, swims upside down underwater; the Pond Skater, 1cm. long which walks over the surface, as does the very thin bodied Water Measurer, about the same size and the sturdier, slightly shorter, Water Cricket. Winged specimens of this last species are only found occasionally.

**Water Beetles.** Many beetle larvae exist in the water. They are not easy to distinguish by the casual observer at this stage in their life cycle, but when adult are easy to separate. Commonest are the black Carnivorous Water Beetle (Great Diving Beetle), 3-4cm. Black with golden brown coloured legs, antennae and lines, which outline the wing cases, head and thorax. This is a fierce predator, attacking and killing prey larger than itself, even small fish. The slightly larger Silver Water Beetle, 4-5cm, black with a silver outline to the wingcases and body segments, has clubbed antennae and feeds on water plants, as do the very active tiny Whirligig

Beetles, 1.5cm sometimes seen in large numbers, swimming in endless circles on the surface in late summer. Other brown, black or striped water beetles may be noticed which need a specialist book to identify them.

## 5. SPIDERS

Spiders are not insects, belonging to the separate sub-phylum Arachnida.

**Water Spiders and Water Mites.** Several species of Water Mite, mostly about 1-2mm long, often bright red or multicoloured, may be noted swimming actively. The commonest are *Diplodontus* and *Hydrarachna* species. They are carnivorous, sucking out the body fluids of their victims through their pointed beaks. The larvae are parasitic on other water insects, dropping off and becoming free-living when mature. Water Spiders are usually of the genus *Argyroneta*. They live beneath the water and construct a weblike airbell in which they store the air they need to breathe, carrying air bubbles down to the nest between their legs.

## 6. MOLLUSCS

**Pond Snails.** The Marsh Snail 20-25mm and the Great Pond Snail 30-55mm, are tall elongated species, with thin, 4-5-whorled shells varying in colour from dark brown to black, with lighter or whitish striae, spiral and transverse on the Marsh Snail and usually only transverse on the Great Pond Snail. The Wandering Pond Snail, varies in size and shape, but is generally rounded with 3-5 whorls, the lowest taking up most of the shell. These all have their openings on the right hand side of the shell. They are also found in slow flowing streams. Another species, the Liver Fluke Snail, 1-2cm, a species of marsh and ditch, which is host to the sheep liver fluke might be found in damp areas living out of the water on wet mud. In the marshy fringes of the Vale pond look for the Salt Marsh Snail or Spire Snail, cone-shaped 6-10mm high, and two smaller species of the same genus, *Hydrobia,* including the Laver Spire Snail. In Guernsey Ram's Horn Snails occur in the streams. The River Limpet has been recorded in two or three places in Guernsey and at Trois Vaux in Alderney.

A narrow elongated shell with 6-7 whorls and a left hand opening sometimes seen in ditches or shallow water, especially on the grass *Glyceria fluitans,* is probably *Aplexa hypnorum*. Others doubtless occur but we have not recorded them. Pfeiffer's Amber Snail has been reported from several marshy places in Guernsey and Mannez pond in Alderney.

All of these species rise to the surface and breathe by means of a lung. They have no operculum to close the open end of the shell and can frequently be seen at the surface with the foot uppermost and a large opening at the side through which the air is drawn in. If disturbed this opening closes with a distinct hiss.

We have not noted any freshwater mussels in Alderney although it is likely that these occur in mud at the bottom of the water in some larger domestic ponds or the quarries and reservoirs. As their survival depends on the larvae attaching themselves to fish and embedding themselves in their skin for about three months, before dropping off to become free living, this lack of sighting is not surprising. In Guernsey four species of Pea Mussels, *Pisidium* spp. 1.5-7mm have been noted both in flowing streams, ponds and lakes.

## Vertebrates.

### 7. FISH

In Guernsey, Stickleback, Eel and Wild Carp are considered to be native, whilst Brown and Rainbow Trout, Rudd, Perch, Mericarp, Grass Carp, Chub, Tench, Roach, Bream and Perch have all been introduced, some probably as long ago as the 9th Century by the Monks in their stewponds and viviers. Several species are abundant in St. Saviour's Reservoir and others will be found in the water-filled quarries to which they have been introduced in more recent times, for the benefit of local anglers. Various "Goldfish" are also to be found in these, probably cleared out from domestic ponds.

The only freshwater fish native to Alderney are the Stickleback found in Corblets Quarry and formerly in the Mill Leat in La Bonne Terre and the pond, now reformed, which existed on Platte Saline until the 1960s, below it and Eels, which were found before the war in the stream near the Nunnery.

Rainbow Trout and Carp have been introduced into Corblets Quarry for the Alderney Angling Club and there were many Goldfish, Golden Orfe, or Carp, large and small, in the pond in Mannez Quarry when it dried up in August 1990. These also were presumably the result of the breeding over many years of fish cleared out of overstocked garden ponds and several thousand were transferred to Corblets to save them. The authors transferred a large bucket full of the smaller ones to ponds in their own garden and another to the small reservoir below the former watermill, until their proposed reclamation scheme for Mannez Pond was agreed by the States and the years of silt had been dug out in September by the Agricultural team. Some were returned to Mannez once the pond was re-established.

Eels were found in the stream emerging at the Nunnery, the only place in the island where fresh water comes into direct contact with the sea in a stream bed. They were apparently quite common in this stream before the last war, the smaller

Elvers were used as bait by the fishermen and a few larger specimens were caught and eaten. They have not been seen for some years.

In Elizabethan times, and for centuries previously, the pond on Longis Common was a well stocked vivier and was, from before 1200, the perquisite of the Church and later of the Crown, represented by the Lieutenant Governors, Fee-farmers or 'Lords of the Manor'. It is not known what fish were there then. On many old maps it is marked as La Mare du Roe, presumably a corruption of Roi, the 'King's pond'. On some 17th and 18th century maps the line of a stream is shown feeding into it from the north and flowing out of it, to the sea on the south-eastern side. Fresh water still runs across the middle area of Longis beach as the tide recedes, frequently in considerable quantity after heavy rain, but there is no discernable stream bed on the common now.

The only native freshwater fish on Sark appear to be Eels, which are found in a number of the wells.

## 8. Birds

All birds, including those living on freshwater will be dealt with in Chapter 11.

Goose Barnacle from Gerard's Herbal 1633

*Chapter 8*

# AMPHIBIANS AND REPTILES

The Bailiwick islands were separated from the continent, before the majority of animals in these groups had reached the area. The only indigenous reptiles found are the Slow-worm, a legless lizard, seen regularly, if infrequently, along the cliffs in Guernsey, Alderney and possibly also in Sark and the Green Lizard (in Guernsey only), found along the cliffs on the SE part near Fermain Bay. This is unknown in Alderney, Sark or England.

There have been rare but unconfirmed reports of Grass Snakes in the last few years. It is likely that these have been imported as pets and were released or lost.

Frogs were recorded in Guernsey in 1862 in Ansted's book, and both the Common and the rare Agile forms are now found. It is not known if they are indigenous or had been introduced earlier. The Smooth Newt has been known in ponds on L'Ancresse and in some quarries since the 1930s, probably introduced from Jersey, where it is common. The authors received a single report of a Newt seen in a garden pond in Alderney in 1995. Toads were apparently introduced to Guernsey, from Jersey in 1953, but the existence of either frogs and toads in Alderney was doubtful before the Second World War. There do not seem to be any frogs or toads on Herm, unless they have been introduced in recent years.

The occasional Toad has been reported since then, almost always from enclosed gardens in the town area and a single specimen of the Jersey Agile Frog was found and identified at Mannez about 1966, by Vic Mendham. Three of these were noted in the same area by the authors in 1989. Frogs are now quite plentiful in Sark, mainly in garden ponds, but Toads have not been recorded.

Probably due to the influx of English settlers with families and the building of garden ponds, frog spawn has been brought into Alderney on a number of occasions and in recent years Common Frogs have been seen regularly around Longis and Mannez ponds, as well as in garden ponds, sometimes found hibernating in the mud at the bottom when they are cleaned and spawn and tadpoles are regularly noticed in the spring.

After the reclamation of part of Longis pond in the autumn of 1989, large quantities of frog spawn and many tadpoles were seen there the following spring and although the pond dried in June, young frogs were seen in the grass around the area in September, which must have come from tadpoles which had matured enough to survive on land before the water dried up.

When the reclamation scheme for Mannez pond was carried out in the summer of 1990, as the Reedmace bed was being cut back, some 60 or more adult frogs were seen, which retreated into the untouched area. These were not identified as to species, but from the description of the workmen could have been a mixture of both Common and Agile frogs.

The status of the Common Frog and possibly also the Agile Frog, as introduced species, seems assured for the future in both Guernsey and Alderney.

Mannez Pond, Alderney

Sark Pond

*Chapter 9*

# LAND MOLLUSCS

The first records of these, are Gosselin's from about 1790, noted in the Introduction to this work. These were followed by lists in Ansted & Latham in 1862, in *Transactions* and in various British technical publications in the late 19th and early 20th centuries. Once again Marquand was to the fore in investigating and recording these.

The principal recent records were made in the 1970s by a number of investigators, mostly members of the Conchological Society. A comprehensive paper will be found in the 1976 *Transactions*. In all 73 species were identified. Only the commonest species have English names. Once again a specialist book is needed to identify most of them.

**Snails.**

In the seaward edges of sand dunes, the Sandhill Snail, *Theba pisana*, a Mediterranean species, 15-18mm and wider than tall, is common. This was probably introduced into Guernsey, from Jersey, by F.C. Lukis in 1860 and arrived in Alderney in the 1930s. Whitish with numerous dark, spiral bands, it can often be seen in great numbers covering Sea Kale, Hogweed, Sea Radish, Sea Holly, Docks and grass stems. It has now colonised small dune areas in Cornwall, Dorset and South Wales. In the dune areas generally, the common Garden Snail, usually about 35mm, the tall, narrow, Pointed Snail, about 20mm high x 5mm, white, streaked with pale brown; the flat glossy shells of several *Oxychilus* species including the 6-7mm. Garlic Snail; the Slippery Moss Snail; Banded Snail; Brown-lipped Snail; and the tiny transparent green 3-5mm Pellucid Glass Snail can be found, together with several other species, some of which are not commonly found in Britain.

In grassland, frequently under stones or bits of wood, look for the Garden Snail, Hairy Snail; and the Banded Snail, 17-20mm, the usually yellowish shell having five dark brown bands. This one is a favourite food of Thrushes.

In woodland, at least a dozen species of tiny snails, 1-3mm, are to be found, often in large numbers.

The "Hedges" of the Channel Islands are usually stone and earth banks densely covered with grass, ivy, primroses and violets. Amongst these look for many tiny snails and also the common Garden Snail and the Chrysalis Snail, another pale, cone-shaped snail about 4mm high. This last is often found amongst ivy on the banks and on stone walls.

**Slugs.**

In grassland, the large, (up to 150mm), Large Black Slug, *Arion ater,* somewhat variable in colour from black, brown and reddish to yellow, with the foot fringe a different colour, is the most common and in gardens, two or three smaller species, the Garden Slug, dark-grey or black with an orange sole being a common crop pest. The Dusky Slug is banded dark-brown/orange, 50-70mm, with a pale sole. These are also found in woodland areas and all three are of the same genus. Sowerby's Slug, up to 75mm, pale grey-brown speckled with black is another common species in these habitats.

Great Green Bush-Cricket

American Cockroach

*Chapter 10*

# INSECTS & SPIDERS

There is a growing interest in Entomology (the study of insects), and the Channel Islands have a rich variety to interest the observer. As in so many other groups, the reader should refer to one of the several field guides available to help identify them.

Unfortunately mowing, overgrazing, spraying with herbicides and insecticides, the removal of flowering trees and shrubs, deprive many species of their sources of food and breeding areas. Insecticides seem particularly lethal to the Hymenoptera, (the ants, bees, and wasps), in fact, this group of animals has a high proportion of endangered species. Many of the bees and wasps are important as pollinators or predators. Some are also parasites or semi-parasites that have developed patterns of behaviour that make them biologically interesting.

Insect conservation is very important not only to maintain their own life cycles but also those of other animals and plants involved in the food chains, and through their role in the fertilisation and propagation of plant species.

Insect conservation can be achieved by maintaining rich and varied habitats in as near their present condition as possible and this needs careful management to maintain the species common in the islands and the less common ones now extinct or nearly so in the U.K. Even planting, or leaving, suitable "wild" areas in domestic gardens can help considerably.

Coastal habitats generally provide precarious conditions for a number of insects threatened for a variety of reasons, not always the result of human activity. Sand dunes are a particularly fragile habitat, easily damaged by trampling and vehicles. As the vegetation wears away the dunes become unstable and subject to wind erosion. Other areas are threatened by housing and other developments such as new marinas, coastal erosion, land reclamation, quarry filling and both air and water pollution.

Insects have three distinct parts to their bodies and six legs, whilst Arachnids have two distinct parts to the body and eight legs. In *Transactions*, between 1882 and 1909, W.A. Luff and other workers recorded most of the insects in the islands and in doing so found many species new to the islands and several new to science. Four of these were named after him. These lists form the basis of all subsequent records in the Bailiwick. Luff founded the Entomological Section of La Société, which, despite intermittent breaks, has continued to thrive and in the last two or three decades, careful recording, particularly of moths trapped at light boxes in recent years, has increased the numbers still further. Members of the group make regular visits to the other islands and their records appear annually in *Transactions*. It is as well to note that the annual section records are principally of butterflies and moths.

There is little space here to do other than record a few of the species seen commonly by daylight, and to make note of those species found in the islands which are rare elsewhere in the British Isles.

## BUTTERFLIES

Their numbers seem to fluctuate considerably from year to year, a fact which is not always easy to relate to the climatic conditions prevailing. By about 1970 some 40 species were known in the Bailiwick, but only a small number of these are common in Guernsey.

Alderney, in spite of a recent increase in the use of herbicides and insecticides, increased clearance of scrubland, and mowing of verges, as well as the recent drought years, is still rich in butterfly life, and during the summer months there are a number of species to be seen in a wide variety of habitats. Sark has a richer population still and the Brimstone, Silver-studded Blue, (now extinct in Guernsey but found on Alderney and Brecqhou) and Hairstreak are quite common there. Herm has these and also the Dark Green Fritillary on the Common. This is also found on Sark, Brecqhou and in large numbers on Jethou, rarely in Guernsey, but not on Alderney. In Alderney and Sark the Glanville Fritillary is common but has greatly declined in Guernsey.

Butterflies always have to make the best use of sunshine. They can have rather a hard time in temperate zones. Their adult life is usually very brief, and they cannot fly or lay their eggs unless they are warm, (body temperature above 28º C), and have sufficient energy to do so. Sometimes due to weather, latitude, or altitude, the females can only lay one fifth of their potential supply of eggs.

Some are able to exploit or trap the sun's heat. The Clouded Yellows raise their temperature by basking on their sides. In this position, the butterfly raises its yellow wings vertically above its back, and so exposes the underside of the hind-wing to the sun. If the butterfly's body temperature begins to exceed 40º C, it repositions itself parallel to the sun's rays to cool down.

The colour of butterflies wings makes them efficient absorbers of heat. Black absorbs radiant heat most effectively, and because the wings are poor conductors, the most effective area for absorption is in the area of the wings nearest to the body. Different species have different amounts of black pigment on the lower underside of the wings, depending on the outside temperature, butterflies in colder regions have more black pigment.

The Large (or Cabbage) Whites have evolved a different system that gives them more control over the rate at which they gain heat. These butterflies take on a different position for raising their temperature, called reflectance basking. The butterflies use their wings as solar energy reflectors, holding them open at an angle, the back oriented towards the sun. Solar radiation reflects off the white upper surface of the wings on to the body. The portion of the wings nearest to the body is black and absorbs most heat. The Cabbage White species are able to control the rate at which they warm up by controlling the angle of their wings. The narrower the angle between the wings, the more heat is reflected and absorbed.

The following species are those more commonly found in the islands, and the reader can best identify them from one of the field guides.

Speckled Wood 4½ cm. Flying late March to October. Feeds on Bramble flowers. Caterpillars feed on grass. Commonest inland species. Has two broods, occasionally three, abundant.

Wall Brown 4½ cm. Found from spring-autumn. Lives in the higher areas, often seen basking with wings open on stone walls near the airport. Caterpillars are green with white dots, and feed on grasses. The butterfly hibernates in the winter. Has two broods, common.

Meadow Brown 5cm. A drab butterfly, common everywhere June-August. Caterpillars feed on grasses. Two broods.

Small Heath 3cm. Flies throughout the summer. Found on high ground, often flying with the Coppers and Blues. Caterpillars are a clear green with 4-6 dark stripes, use grasses for food. The butterflies hibernate over winter. Abundant.

Grayling 5½ cm. Found on heath or grass on high ground, near the coast. Flies only a short distance and then settles, usually with closed wings. Active July and August. The caterpillar feeds on grasses, hibernates, and completes its growth in the spring. Common.

Glanville Fritillary 4cm. Seen usually in May and June and again in August in some years, mostly on the cliffs. This is a very rare butterfly, found only in the Isle of Wight in England, but common here. Caterpillars feed on Ribwort and Buck's-Horn plantain.

Small Tortoiseshell 4cm. A very common resident. Flies all summer, but may be seen as early as February and as late as December. Caterpillars black and spiky, and feed on Nettles. They often hibernate, coming into houses for protection, especially the late summer third brood.

Red Admiral 5½ cm. It is also a migrant, and very common in the islands from May to October. The caterpillars live singly in silk-like containers on Nettles and Thistles. The adults favour Buddleia and Hemp Agrimony. There is only one brood a year.

Painted Lady 5½ cm. This migrant produces two broods a year, June and August/September. The spiky caterpillars feed mainly on Thistles. Abundant some years, rare in others.

Peacock 6cm. A hibernating resident, seen here as early as February or March, but mainly July to September, often on Buddleia and other garden flowers.

Increasing in Guernsey. Common at Mannez in Alderney. Caterpillars feed on Stinging Nettles May to July. Common in some years.

Large White 6cm. Two broods a year, flies May-September. Population often increased by migrants from France. Caterpillars are green, yellow and black, and live on Brassicas and Nasturtiums. These do a lot of damage in Gardens. Common.

Small White 4½ cm. Flies March to October. Caterpillars are green, and live on Brassicas and Nasturtiums. Sometimes has three broods. Very common.

Green-veined White 4½ cm. Seen March to October. The green caterpillars feed on cructfers like Charlock, usually in damp places. Quite common.

Clouded Yellow 5cm. This migrant from Central and Southern Europe is often found during the summer. Although they are fairly uncommon in Alderney, many were reported in 1990. Caterpillars green with a yellow stripe on either side. They feed on Clovers and other leguminous (pea-family) plants.

Green Hairstreak 2½ cm. There is a single brood which flies in May and June. Fairly widespread in rough grassy or scrubby places. The caterpillars are pale green, and feed on Bird's-foot Trefoil, Broom, Gorse and Heather. Frequent in most years.

Small Copper 3cm. They fly from May to October in grassy areas, especially round the coast. The caterpillar is green with a dark head, and lives on Sorrel and Dock. Two broods. Quite common.

Brown Argus 2½ cm. Often flying from April to September or October with the Common Blue and Small Copper. The caterpillar feeds on Stork's-bill. Fairly common.

Common Blue 3½ cm. This is the commonest of the European blues and flies from April in grassy areas. It is a variable species. The male has violet-blue upper sides to the wings with a narrow white edge. The female can be darker blue with marginal orange spots, or brown with a varied amount of blue at the base of the wings. The caterpillars feed on leguminous plants. Double brooded, abundant.

Holly Blue 3cm. The male is a shining light blue, with a narrow black border. The females have black tips to their wings. This species has two broods, April/May and July/August. In spring the caterpillars feed on the buds of Holly, and the later brood on the buds of Ivy. Common some years, scarce in others.

In Alderney, the Brimstone and the Silver-Studded Blue were reported around Platte Saline and the Zig-Zag in 1990, but they are uncommon. The Brimstone hibernates and may be one of the earliest seen in the spring. The Comma is seen occasionally early or late in the year. Berger's Clouded Yellow and Pale Clouded Yellow, 5cm. Both these species fly from May to September. The caterpillars are green with yellow lines and black spots. They feed on Vetches and other leguminous plants. (These are rare). The Gatekeeper, common in Sark, was recorded for the first time in Alderney by the authors in 1995, seen in some numbers along the east coast.

Butterflies are among the most colourful and popular members of the insect world. Many perform a courtship display; their initial attention is by sight, and this is followed by a scent, the males producing more than the females. This scent is produced by special scales scattered over the wings. The female lays its fertilised eggs, using sense organs on the head and feet to make sure they are laid on the correct food-plant for the caterpillars. They are declining rapidly in many places in Britain and Europe.

We must be careful to maintain good management of our areas of heath and scrub, to avoid the same fate overtaking them here.

## MOTHS

The casual observer will probably only encounter the small number of day-flying moths and micro-moths, or notice the occasional large species in their resting state.

Amongst these, more commonly seen on most of the islands, and more easily recognisable, will be;

The Jersey Tiger, in both red and yellow under-winged forms, common here July to September, but unusual in Britain; the Garden Tiger, less common, in July and August; the smaller Cream-spot Tiger, in May-June; Five and Six-spot Burnets, with the 5-spot abundant in July and early August; Cinnabar, common late May-July; the Silver Y, a common migrant often seen in large numbers on the heathland in August; Humming-bird Hawk, (usually noted around Honeysuckle); Gypsy; Magpie, common in July and August; Brimstone Moth, common April to October; Great Eggar and Oak Eggar; Drinker, common on grassland in July and August; the Yellow or Straw Belle, common in May/June and again August/September in drier years; and the Small Ermel, whose caterpillars live communally in web-like tents, and completely defoliate the Blackthorn around the cliffs in many years.

A common sight on the outside of lighted windows at night is the distinctive White Plume Moth, which at rest looks like a pure white letter T.

A list of 43 moths, not previously recorded from Alderney, will be found in the 1970 *Transactions*.

The larger-sized moths seen may include;

The Emperor, Europe's largest moth, an exclusively night flying moth, the female of which is sometimes seen resting on short turf in April and May in the daytime; Privet Hawk in June-July and Convolvulus Hawk, the female of which is nearly twice the size of the male, mid-summer-mid-autumn, particularly in drought years, are all variable in numbers.

## DRAGONFLIES & DAMSELFLIES

Sixteen breeding species of Dragonfly have been recorded in Guernsey, of which nine have been recorded in Alderney, with five known to breed there. Only one species has been noted in Sark and two in Herm. It would be tragic to see any further decline or possible loss of these insects, therefore it is important to provide adequate habitats, and maintain those already established.

Insects have declined by a third since the second world war because of agricultural changes, and rural development. Dragonflies and Damselflies, have fared particularly badly because of their dependence on water. Their eggs are laid beneath the surface of water in ponds and lakes in the summer.

Dragonflies are among the most ancient of living creatures. In Bolsover in Derbyshire, Palæozoic rocks from the 350 million year-old Devonian period have been found to contain fossils of enormous dragonflies with wing spans of 28 inches. They therefore pre-date Pterodactyls by 100 million years and birds by 150 million.

Dragonflies can register speeds of 40mph. The wings of most insects work as two pairs, but those of dragonflies are independent of one another. They can fly forwards, sideways, and upside down and can even take off backwards, they are superb acrobats.

There is plenty of open water with emergent vegetation in Guernsey, but their breeding spots in Alderney are somewhat restricted. Longis and Mannez ponds and Corblets Quarry, when it is full, are the best spots, with the many garden ponds playing a secondary role. After hatching swarms are sometimes seen in the vicinity of the three major sites, with the Emperor Dragonfly prevalent for a day or two on the dunes behind the Targets, a few yards from the sea at the eastern end of Longis Bay.

Those most likely to be seen are;

The Blue-tailed and Southern Emerald Damselflies, and the Common Darter and Emperor Dragonflies.

## GRASSHOPPERS AND CRICKETS

There are a good many grasshoppers, some of which are best distinguished by their sounds, but unfortunately only by the expert.

The most prominent and easily identified in this group is the Great Green Bush-Cricket, a spectacular brilliant green insect, the female up to 10cm. long, with feelers as long again. The male is a little more than half that. Quite frequent amongst brambles, but never in large numbers. In Guernsey there is a smaller coastal Grey Bush Cricket, the Channel Island species being distinct from the British one. Another Bush Cricket, the Long-winged Conehead is common in long grass in Guernsey, Alderney and Sark, whilst the Speckled Bush Cricket is found in Guernsey and Crevichon. The largely nocturnal Mole-cricket is occasionally found in damp areas especially along the banks of streams.

Of the smaller species, by far the most common in drier areas is the Meadow Grasshopper, the only one of the several common species which cannot fly. It is generally green in colour, whilst the larger Common Field Grasshopper is usually brown. Along the cliff paths, look for the Blue-winged Grasshopper, another Channel and Scilly Isles species. The yellow-grey House Cricket is sometimes found in older houses.

## BEES & WASPS

There are at least 16 species of Bumble Bee present amongst the various islands, most of which make their own burrows below ground, but one of which *Bombus lapidarus* a black bee with a red tail uses mouse holes.

Amongst the heather will be noticed the pale yellow-brown *B. muscorum* and the beautiful *B. smithianus* with red-brown thorax, yellow abdomen and shiny black remainder. This species appears identical to the one found in the Scilly Isles, and is only found in Alderney. *B. pascuorum* is brown and common everywhere, whilst two similar very large bees, with white tails and yellow-banded thorax will be noticed, *B. terrestris* and *B. leucorum*.

Altogether 156 species of bees, many of them minute and parasitic have been recorded in the islands. Each island has a number of species that have not so far been noted in the others, but a total of 85 are recorded from Guernsey, 70 from Alderney, 40 from Sark and 36 from Herm.

Cuckoo bees which kill the queen cell, and then lay their eggs in other bees' nests, a leaf-cutter bee, flower bees of the *Anthropora* genus, and the burrows of several mining bees probably of the *Andrena* species are particularly common around the cliffs above Telegraph Bay, Alderney, and on Burhou. The solitary bee, *Colletes halophilus* makes its multi-celled burrows in sandy soil near the coast. It has a golden-brown thorax, and a black/fawn-striped rear. *Hallictus* species also nest in the ground.

The few honey bees seen will probably be from hives.

A total of 12 species of wasp have been recorded (11, 10, 4 and 2 respectively from the four main islands) and 36 Sand-wasps (30, 26, 7 and 6 respectively).

The Common, and German wasps, *Vespula vulgaris* and *V. germanica* are frequently seen in late summer. The Sand-digger Wasps may be confused with the several species of Hoverflies to be seen. Hornets are exceedingly rare or their records even doubtful.

## ANTS

There are at least 24 species of black, red, yellow and wood, ant, including two species found here, but not in Britain, which can only be distinguished by an expert. 20 species have been recorded from Guernsey, 11 from Alderney, 14 from

Sark and 9 from Herm. All four islands also have a small *Plagiolepis* species around the base of the cliffs, which is not found in Britain.

Ants swarm in large numbers in July and August, when conditions are right, most colonies of the same species swarming at the same time, often to the great concern of visitors.

## BEETLES, FLIES, etc.

Beetles form the largest group of all the insect orders. A total of 651 species are recorded in Guernsey, a large proportion of which will probably be found in the other islands. These include Ground beetles e.g. the Violet Ground Beetle, Burying or Sexton beetles, Rove beetles such as the Devil's Coach Horse, Stag, Chafer, Leaf, Longhorn and Dung Beetles. Weevils are included in this group as are Ladybirds. Some 45 species of these are known in Britain and Northern Europe. Both larvae and adults feed on aphids and scale insects. The yellow eggs are laid in the vicinity of a colony of aphids. The larvae are blue-black with yellow spots and each consumes hundreds of aphids during its 3-week larval phase. They then pupate in a sheltered place on the plant and emerge as adults six days later. Many species are red with black spots, the most commonly found is probably the 7-spot, but others are yellow or orange with darker spots or splodges on the elytra.

The Cockchafer beetle or May-bug, stripy light brown in colour, is responsible for cutting holes in the leaves of many plants. Their larvae live in the soil and cause much damage to crop roots. Rose Chafer beetles, bright green in colour, are responsible for cutting holes in the leaves of roses and have destructive larvae which feed on decaying wood. Both are common throughout the islands. Keep a special lookout for another leaf-beetle, the bright green Tortoise Beetles, *Cassida rubiginosa*, about 0.5-1cm long, with very short stubby legs.

Many aphids, (most commonly greenfly and blackfly) have been noted. These mate in the autumn and the females give birth to live young in the spring, usually numbering about 50. There are also several species of Gall-wasp whose activities produce galls varying from the numerous small rounded galls on the back of the leaves of oak and other trees, through the marble galls often seen on oak, including our common Evergreen Oak, to the spectacular 'Robin's Pincushion' found from time to time on wild roses.

Other types of insect to be seen include; Silverfish, Springtails, Cockroaches, Earwigs, Shieldbugs (163 species locally), Squashbugs, Froghoppers, Leafhoppers, Thrips and Whitefly.

The 220 Fly species recorded in the islands include Horse, Robber, House, Saw and Ichneumon flies. A number of species of Hoverfly will be noted, the largest of which is *Volucella zonaria*. Many species of these have aphid-eating larvae and lay their eggs close to a colony of aphids, so that the blind, legless larvae are surrounded by food. The adult hoverflies feed on pollen, nectar and honeydew and are valuable flower pollinators.

Of the larger, mostly black, beetles, those seen most frequently are;

The Bloody-nosed Beetle, Britain's largest leaf beetle; the Minotaur Beetle, which lives on rabbit droppings which it buries as much as 150cm deep in sandy soils; the Lesser Stag Beetle; and Oil Beetles.

## SPIDERS

Marquand listed 201 species of Arachnida in the Bailiwick in 1907 which included 190 species of spider, a number of them continental in origin and 11 not found in Britain. Lists for Alderney were published in the 1899 and 1902 *Transactions* and at the latter date numbered 69 species out of the 142 then recorded for the whole of the Channel Islands. An 1894 paper on Sark listed 83 for that island. A further paper was published by W.S. Bristowe in the 1929 *Transactions* (p.407). He added 2 species to the Guernsey list and 10 to the Sark list, although he also added 24 to the small number (17) previously recorded from Jersey, he did not apparently visit Alderney or Herm. 1973 *Transactions* contains the complete list by J.A. Guerin, who had added another 7 species to the total, all from Guernsey. There are doubtless others still to be found, but nothing has been published in the succeeding years.

Some of those most likely to be noticed on casual observation are; the Orb-web Spiders, Garden Spiders, House Spiders, Crab Spiders and hunting spiders such as the Wolf Spiders.

Harvestmen although common and of similar appearance are not true spiders. They have a single body unit with two eyes on a turret on top. They are basically scavengers and do not produce silk.

Although neither Insects nor Spiders this seems a convenient place to mention three other types of small creature which are frequently seen.

## ARTHROPODS

Centipedes, which have one pair of legs to each body segment and Millipedes which have two pairs are both members of this group.

The commonest centipede is *Necrophloeophagus longicornis* which has 49 or 51 pairs of legs.

## LAND CRUSTACEA

Woodlice of several species are widespread.

*Chapter 11*

# BIRDS

Records of birds in the Bailiwick have been kept for more than a century, the first published work being Cecil Smith's *Birds of Guernsey and the Neighbouring Islands* in 1879. There are many references since 1889 in a number of special reports in *Transactions* and various details about birds ringed and new or rare species, recorded in each of the islands, are printed in the Annual Reports of the Ornithological Section of La Société Guernesiaise. An updated list appeared in the 1961 volume. Alderney records are published monthly in *The Alderney Journal*, and annually in the Alderney Society *Bulletin*.

The most recent book, Roderick Dobson's *Birds of the Channel Islands* published in 1952 is long out of print, but two works by Mike Hill on the Breeding Seabirds (1991 & 1993) and Nick Milton's book *The Red Data Book Birds of the Channel Islands* (1992) are still available. A.J. Bisson published privately in 1989 *A List of the Birds of Guernsey; also checklist of the Birds of the Channel Islands*. In 1974 F.R.G. Rountree produced *Birds of Sark* for the Sark Ornithological Committee and in the same year a checklist for Alderney, by Peter Conder was published by the Alderney Society. This was updated by Marie Louise Mendham with all records since then included and the new *List of the Birds of Alderney*, published by the Society in 1990, is available from the Alderney Museum. The Sark list was updated by a *Supplement* in 1991.

The reader is referred to these for detailed lists, but it is relevant to mention some of the special birds in this chapter. Milton's survey of Red Data Book Birds in 1992, listed the following endangered species found in Guernsey, Alderney and Sark, often seen as passage migrants;

Manx Shearwater, (breeding on Sark, Burhou and Jethou); Storm Petrel, (breeding round Alderney and Sark); Gannet, (Alderney's breeding colonies are of national importance); Brent Goose, (Winter visitor, with a large flock usually on Herm); Peregrine, (regular visitor); Ringed Plover, (important winter visitor to Guernsey and occasional breeder in Guernsey and Alderney); Grey Plover, (occasional Winter visitor in Guernsey and Alderney); Sanderling, Bar-tailed Godwit, Redshank, Turnstone, (Winter numbers important in Guernsey, Common in Alderney, rare in Sark); Sandwich Tern, Barn Owl, (breed in small numbers in all three islands); Cetti's Warbler, (rare summer visitor in Guernsey and Alderney, has bred in Sark); Dartford Warbler, (still breeding in Guernsey, and now returning to Alderney and Sark after the 1987 hurricane decimated its numbers); Serin, (rare summer visitor); Cirl Bunting (a very rare visitor).

The same survey also lists some "Candidate species", generally declining and thus for possible inclusion at a later date; Herring Gull, (still common in the islands); Puffin, (still breeding in much reduced numbers); Stonechat, (a few recent breeding records); Linnet, (abundant resident and migrant in Guernsey, common as both in Alderney, uncommon resident but common passage migrant in Sark. No breeding figures available).

Finally, species of special local interest in the islands; Fulmar; (breeds in Alderney and Herm); Cormorant, (not very common, but breeding in small numbers); Shag, (common and breeding on rocks and reefs all round the islands. Most small offshore emergent rocks carry their quota, frequently seen with wings outstretched to dry); Common Tern, (not all that common but breeding on Omptolle off Guernsey, the Brehon Tower in the Little Russel channel and Alderney); and the Short-toed Treecreeper, (this last unique to the CIs, within the British Isles, having a more curved bill and shorter toes than the British species).

The islands are on the edge of the winter and spring migratory routes and at these times a number of rare visitors drop in for a day or two, or even a few weeks, whilst more common species such as Lapwing, Fieldfare and Redwing, (these especially during severe weather further north), Black-throated and Great Northern Divers, Redshank, Curlew and Whimbrel, Turnstone, Little Ringed Plover and other smaller waders, may either stay as winter visitors, drop down for a rest and feed, or be seen in large numbers flying past the cliffs on their way south or north. The best points to view these in passing are from Lihou Island and the cliffs at Pleinmont, both in Guernsey. A few, such as the Kentish Plover breed regularly in Guernsey, Alderney and Herm, although only in small numbers. The airports in Guernsey and Alderney are good places to see flocks of many migrating wildfowl.

Heathlands on commons and cliffs in all of the islands are important sites for a variety of species, and good places for observers at most times of the year.

In Guernsey one of the most important inland sites for breeding birds is the Marais area of St. Sampson. Protected for many years against shooters, with large reed beds and small open water areas, several small warblers, various ducks, Kingfishers, Wagtails, Moorhens, etc. breed here. It is also a favourite haunt for many winter visitors including Snipe, Water Rail and Ruff. Other sites such as L'Erée and La Grande Mare have to some extent been affected by recent housing and hotel development, but La Société's reserves at Les Vicheries (Clare Mare) and Vale Pond have been developed to provide improved habitats for all these species.

About 50 species of sea-birds and waders have been recorded round the islands and Alderney has had, since about 1945, two breeding colonies of Gannets. These are sited on Ortac a stack between Burhou and The Casquets, where a single nest was first found in 1940, and on Les Étacs or the Garden Rocks a couple of hundred yards offshore at the Giffoine. The Gannets begin to return towards the end of January and depart in late July or August, when the young are strong enough to fly great distances. A few linger into September or even October. The two colonies now number nearly 5,000 nests.

Fulmars started to breed on Alderney's cliffs about 1975 and are now well established in several sites. The Little Auk breeds on L'Etac de la Quoire and on Burhou.

The Puffin, present in many thousands until the 1960's has suffered a decline in population due to a variety of reasons, throughout much of its southern range and a few years ago was down to less than 100 pairs on Burhou. It is now increasing slowly, with about 300 pairs in 1989 and is now also established on the cliffs of Alderney itself, in Hannaine Bay, in small numbers. It also breeds on the cliffs of Herm, on Galeux and Godin, two of Les Amfroques ('The Humps') to the north of Herm and on Sark.

In the 1960s Burhou had possibly the most important breeding colony of Storm Petrels in the world and over 1,000 were ringed in 1962, the total reaching almost 3,000 by 1965. The colony has suffered a severe decline since and at least some of this is due to predation by the Great Black-backed Gull.

Guillemots and Razorbills also breed on the off-shore stacks and there are now a number of small colonies of the Common Tern, especially on Fort Hommeaux Florains and the Brehon Tower. A Kittiwake colony was first noted on Coque Lihou in the summer of 1986 and has thrived, with further nests now found on the nearby cliffs of Alderney.

About ten species of gull are recorded in the Bailiwick, with Herring, Great and Lesser Black-backed and Black-headed being the common ones, the last named being generally a winter visitor only, departing soon after developing its black-head breeding plumage.

Winter visitors include amongst the larger birds, Brent Geese in small numbers for a day or two most years around St. Saviour's Reservoir and in Alderney, whilst a flock numbering as many as 100 usually overwinters in Herm. Occasional visits from other geese and rarely Mute Swans. A pair, a female and an immature bird, stayed for a week or two in Corblets Quarry in Alderney in 1988 and a single male stayed there for several months in 1989 until it died. A male Black Swan spent about 10 days in Crabby and Braye Bays in August 1991 and another spent a week at Platte Saline in 1994. Two specimens of White-tailed Eagles were shot in the island in the 1890s, one on Burhou. Individual birds of several species of Grebe and Diver are seen during most years, more commonly at Braye and Longis

Bays, St. Saviour's Reservoir and the Vale Pond. Shelduck, Tufted Duck, Wigeon and Pochard have been noted a few times, whilst Teal are frequent winter visitors.

Many migrant bird species are recorded in the spring and autumn passages from Lihou island. A number of waders and seabirds such as Common Sandpiper, Grey Plover, Dunlin, several species of Grebes and Divers, several species of geese and ducks, including Eider, Common Scoter and Red-breasted Merganser, with Brent Geese feeding on the Zostera in the braye between Lihou and Guernsey. Land-based birds seen then include Wheatears, (including the larger Greenland Wheatear), Chiff-chaff and Willow Warbler, Pied Flycatcher, Whinchat, Redstart and Black Redstart.

About 250 species of land birds are recorded in the Bailiwick. The Dartford Warbler regularly bred in small numbers (15-20 pairs) in Alderney until the severe winter of 1984/5. Since then and later, following the hurricane of October 1987, which reduced its numbers further, it has not been known to breed, although individuals were sometimes seen. In 1993 and 1994 the numbers had increased and pairs were seen at Longis, Tourgis and along the south cliffs. It has also bred on the south cliffs in Guernsey and in Sark since the early 1960s. Two other small birds, the Wren and the Dunnock, breed in considerable numbers. The Stonechat had its breeding numbers decimated in the hurricane, but in 1990 several nesting pairs were noted and it was seen in a number of places by observers during 1994.

The Collared Dove, a Mediterranean species, first began to breed in Guernsey in the 1950s and in Alderney in 1965 and is now present in some numbers in all the main islands, breeding regularly. Rock Doves and Stock Doves breed in small numbers, particularly on the south cliffs, whilst large migrant flocks of Turtle Doves are seen in most years. Ravens breed in small numbers on the cliffs and in recent years Jackdaws have been breeding on the south cliffs too. Magpies, common, even abundant, in Guernsey and Jersey are virtually unknown in Alderney, whilst Jays are very rare there, usually in passage. There are a number of Rookeries in Guernsey. There are probably five or six resident pairs of Barn Owls in Guernsey, one pair in Sark and two or possibly three resident pairs in Alderney. Two dead, well fledged young were found there during 1990 and again in 1994. Post mortem on the last pair revealed that they had a massive mite infestation and had starved to death. A Snowy Owl spent several weeks in Alderney in 1992/3, during which time it apparently made a short visit to Guernsey and then returned.

The Swift, House Martin and Swallow are summer breeding residents, with Swallows in considerable numbers. Sand Martins are rare. Of the finches, Chiff-chaff, Chaffinch, Greenfinch, Goldfinch and Linnet are common, whilst Bullfinch and Hawfinch are infrequent. They all breed in the islands, except possibly the Linnet. Robin, Blackbird, Thrush and Starling also breed here, their numbers all being swelled by winter migration. Fieldfare, Redwing and Redstart are all winter residents. House Sparrow and Dunnock are common, as are Blue Tits and Great Tits. White Wagtail, a continental variant of the Pied Wagtail, are frequent and breed here, whilst Pied, Grey and occasionally Yellow Wagtails are autumn and winter visitors.

Considerable numbers of Cuckoos come in the spring each year. Most years see visits from the Hoopoe and Herons are frequent visitors, usually the Grey, (look for them round most of the open freshwater areas in Guernsey and Alderney and round the flatter rocky shores), but including occasionally the Purple Heron. For many years Longis Pond, a favourite spot for many small warblers in Alderney's only reed bed, was so overgrown as to present no open water. Partial clearance in the autumn of 1989, a process intended to be extended annually for the succeeding five years, restored open water. Unfortunately, the need for water for the island supplies in two drought years 1989/90, caused the boreholes on the common to be brought into use and rapidly lowered the water table causing the pond to dry up again. In early March 1991 there was about two feet of water there, with frog spawn and Water Crowfoot present, but pumping started again and it dried up in about ten days. This was followed by another dry summer in 1991. The winter of 1992/3 filled it again and some water remained throughout the year. The very wet autumn of 1993 followed by considerable rainfall in the summer of 1994 and greatly reduced pumping, restored the pond to something like its former area, albeit badly overgrown round the margins. A pair of Coots and a pair of Moorhens nested there. Heavy rain in November and December 1994 and January, February and early March 1995 filled the pond to overflowing and turned the area of common behind the sea wall into a lake. Coots, Moorhens and Mallard bred there in 1995. This seems likely to assure its continued open-water status, at least for the next year or two.

Currently the freshwater species in Alderney are only represented by a few pairs of Moorhen, mostly in the ponds and stream in Rose Farm valley and a pair at Mannez pond. Coots are not common either. This pond also dried up in 1990 for the first time for many years and one of the authors organised a rescue operation for the several thousand small carp/goldfish found as the waters receded. The States carried out a reclamation scheme under his direction when the accumulated silt and much of the encroaching vegetation was removed from the rock base and the banks heightened to give a greater depth of water in future. This filled to the brim during the winter of 1990/91, giving greater hope for it retaining some of the much larger volume of water in future droughts and some of the fish were returned in the spring. Despite the dry summer of 1991 reducing the level considerably it was not in danger of drying up again and has maintained a good level of water throughout the year since that time. Water Rail are seen most years in the stream flowing down Le Vallée especially at the Platte Saline end. Kingfishers are sometimes seen round the harbour and at garden ponds.

Ducks are occasional visitors to the island, migrant flocks of Mallard becoming increasingly frequent in the last few years, but in general only feral and domestic pairs have been known to breed. One Mallard spent the autumn and winter of 1990/91 in Little Crabby harbour. The wet winter of 1993/4 restored the pond on Platte Saline for the first time in many years and a Mallard hatched nine and reared seven there in 1994. Two pairs bred there in 1995 and Teal were seen on several occasions. In Rose Farm valley the owner has also brought in some Black Swans, Mandarin Ducks and other exotic birds which breed on the ponds there.

Some Peacocks were brought to Alderney many years ago, they have survived, raised a few young and after a long sojourn in the Longis Road area, wandered down to Platte Saline, about 1988/9, where they spent much time at Watermill Farm for a couple of years. A group of four first visited the authors' garden near there on 16th March 1991 and came most mornings for several weeks. They later moved to another location and, after many complaints from local residents about the noise they made in their gardens early in the morning, are now back in captivity at Picaterre Farm.

Grey Partridges, Pheasants and Golden Pheasants have been introduced and wild specimens will be seen from time to time in several parts of the island, whilst Woodcock and Snipe are frequent migrants, usually only in small numbers.

The principal resident raptor in the islands is the Kestrel with many breeding pairs. Sparrow Hawks, Merlin and Peregrine Falcons are seen quite frequently and may breed. There are occasional sightings of Marsh and Hen Harriers and Buzzards, these species usually only staying for a few days at a time. The airports are favourite spots for these. The Hobby has also been recorded.

There is some variation between the islands, of the species seen today, or recorded in the past. This is in many cases due to a difference in the available habitats, with Guernsey being the only island in the Bailiwick with any significant marshy, or open freshwater areas. The larger island is also of more importance for winter residents and also during the autumn and spring migrations, when it attracts a wider range of species, both waders and passerines, often with far greater numbers of each species.

There are however a number of differences, less easy to explain. For example, Magpies are common in all of the Channel Islands except Alderney, where they have rarely been recorded at all and are not resident. Their numbers have increased significantly in Jersey and Guernsey in recent years. The Jay is also rarely seen in Alderney, whilst Crows appear to be far more common there than in Sark.

*Chapter 12*

# LAND MAMMALS

Early isolation of the islands from the mainland of Europe not only prevented many species from reaching them in their northward and westward migrations, but also allowed those already present to develop individual characteristics which often separate them from their nearest relatives in either Europe or Britain. The same geological events caused all of the larger animals then present to be hunted to extinction millenia ago.

Today the range of species present is very small. Guernsey has fourteen, (including the Stoat and the Weasel) and Alderney eleven mammals in the wild, but, apart from a few feral domestic cats on the cliffs, there are no major carnivorous species at all.

### Farm Animals

Sheep in small numbers, a few pigs, goats (look out especially for the unusual and beautiful, long-haired, Golden Guernsey Goat) and horses, a herd of imported deer at La Chêne in Guernsey and cattle comprising the dairy herds of Guernsey Cows will be seen.

### The Guernsey Cow

Some cows are still tethered following the ancient island custom and law, but increasingly, with the recent erection of fences, are allowed free within the enclosures. They are thought to have derived from two French breeds brought in by the monks centuries ago. They developed a totally different appearance from the smaller cattle in Jersey and from 1819 the importation of cattle from outside, except for slaughter was forbidden.

Selective breeding since then has produced the now famous cow, high yielding, with rich yellow milk with a high butterfat content. The fat of the slaughtered animal is also yellow. Today all the cows in the Bailiwick are of the same breed.

### The Alderney Cow

The Alderney breed of cattle, which was always very closely related to the Guernsey, only existed as a separate pure strain in the 19th century and up to 1940. Pure Alderneys were in great demand in both England and America around the turn of the century when a healthy and profitable export trade developed. An Alderney Agricultural Society was formed in the 1880s, and was later granted the title "Royal". A Pedigree Register was set up and the Society held an annual cattle and a separate Bull show for many years, into the 1930s. Buyers came from all over, but especially from Guernsey, to purchase them. Laws were introduced to prevent any other breed being imported or any crosses made. The Alderney cattle were generally slightly smaller than the Guernsey, exhibited a number of minor points of difference to the show judges and the milk had a higher butterfat content. When the island was evacuated in 1940, the bulls were almost all slaughtered before the inhabitants left and those cows and calves which were left were transferred to Guernsey during the following week before the German troops arrived. They became mixed with the Guernsey cows shortly after and by 1945 the Alderney as a pure breed had ceased to exist.

After the war, the mixture of Jersey, Guernsey and French cattle brought in by the Germans was either removed from the island or slaughtered for meat and the island was restocked with pure-bred Guernsey cattle, brought from both Guernsey and English herds. To preserve the purity of the Guernsey strain, the laws of the islands still do not permit the presence of any uncastrated male calf except for those of pure, registered Guernsey cattle. An outbreak of Foot-and-mouth disease in Alderney in 1969 almost wiped out these animals and further batches of Guernsey cattle were brought in to replace them. Several of the smaller farmers ceased to keep cows at this time and there are now only two herds. The Royal Alderney Agricultural Society was also disbanded about this time, as the shows attracted few entries and the cattle had all been registered in the Guernsey Herd Book for many years.

These replacements were the ancestors of most of today's two remaining herds. Since about 1989 a few cross bred bullocks or heifers have been brought in for meat, but must be slaughtered by the age of two and are not permitted to breed. The difficulties and cost of importing calves and possibly also of exporting the finished animal or carcass if a local market for the meat cannot be found, ensures that this trade is only minimal.

Sark and Herm both have herds of Guernsey cattle, sufficient for the needs of the island, whilst excess Herm milk is sent daily to the Guernsey States Dairy for processing.

### Wild Animals

**The Rabbit** was possibly introduced in Roman times, but more probably in the 12th Century and is common in Guernsey. There it is to a large extent controlled by 'The Shooters', the season starting on 1st October, and is not the pest that it has become in Alderney and Herm. Myxomatosis has also had a drastic effect on reducing numbers and seems to reappear every time numbers increase greatly. It is also preyed on by **Stoats** which, although now rare, are sometimes seen on the South cliffs. **Weasels,** mentioned in Ansted, have not been recorded in recent years. These are both absent from the other islands and there are no foxes or badgers anywhere in the Bailiwick.

The rabbit has a chequered history in its relationship with the inhabitants of Alderney, which at various times brought them into dispute with the Seigneur over the damage done by rabbits from the Mannez Garenne and on the Island of Burhou.

An ordinance was introduced on 18th January 1773 to prevent non-residents bringing in guns, ferrets or dogs to hunt them, presumably to conserve stocks for the local inhabitants and in Victorian times the troops and government workers, had so depleted their numbers that many were imported and released on Essex Hill. A newspaper report in 1895 noted that rabbits had almost been exterminated by ferreting and the following year a great island 'sportsman', Lionel Langlois wrote that; 'rabbits are as scarce as woodcock'. Some of the old place names of the islands are associated with words used in connection with hunting rabbits.

Rabbits have had a considerable fluctuation in their numbers in recent years due to periodic recurrence of myxomatosis, introduced in the 1950's, but continue to dominate the animal scene with their presence. At a number of places in Alderney one often encounters very dark, or pure black specimens, presumably a result of crossing with escaped domestic pets at some time in the past, although the theory has been put forward that these are a natural wild form, with less natural camouflage than the usual dappled brown animals, which have survived because of the absence of foxes or other large predators. These figure on the 1994 Alderney definitive stamp issue. Black rabbits were also quite common in Herm in the early part of this century.

**Hares** were present in Guernsey until the middle of the 19th Century.

**Hedgehogs,** of the usual brown variety, are common in Guernsey. It is probable that they were introduced prior to 1850, but when is not certain. There are reports that they were present in Alderney in the early 1900s, but had all disappeared by the end of the Great War. They were not found again in the island before the Second World War as far as we can trace, (although there is a rumour that the pre-war specimens were all devoured during the German Occupation) and they were almost certainly introduced since the war, probably in the early 1960s. They have thrived, with no natural predators and amongst them are considerable numbers of a pale blond species, with dark eyes and light brown nose and feet, uncommon elsewhere. These are also shown on the 1994 stamp issue. Occasional albino specimens are seen with pink eyes, nose and feet. There is also an interesting Alderney story, that the apparent freedom of Alderney hedgehogs from the fleas which so heavily infest most English specimens, is because the first imported pair came from Harrod's.

A survey conducted in 1993 by a team under Dr. Pat Morris marked and tracked 67 of Alderney's hedgehogs using tiny transmitters and DF equipment. They noted a greater proportion of dark specimens (about 3:1) at the western end of the island, with no blond specimens found in the airport area. There were no fleas on any of those captured. In the authors' garden at Platte Saline, hedgehogs of all sizes are regularly rescued from their swimming pool cover in the summer and seem to be of roughly equal numbers of each type.

**Mole**

Common in Alderney, but perhaps a little less so in the very sandy eastern and northern parts, the Mole is not found in Guernsey, Sark or Herm, those islands having become detached from the continent before the mole migrated so far west. Their numbers increased considerably in 1993 and 1994, enough to make them a pest in some gardens, especially at Platte Saline and Longis which they had not previously colonised in any great numbers. Mole is also shown on the current Alderney Stamps.

**Rodents**

The **Black** or **Ship's Rat,** responsible for the spread of the plague in the middle ages, was the only rat found until the 18th Century and was also probably introduced by human agency. What was probably one of the last surviving colonies was to be found on the foreshore in front of The Arsenal, Alderney in the 1960's, where considerable numbers were present when it was in use as a meat processing factory. These had not been specially noticed for some years until a comprehensive attack on vermin was introduced by The States Agricultural Committee in 1987, when specimens were noted by the rodent operator. These were not examined in detail and might have been a darker colour form of the brown rat. The black rat has a much longer tail and rounder ears than the brown.

Four specimens were trapped on the Grande Blaye above the South cliffs in January 1994 and identified as this species. Later in an attempt to reduce the large rat population caused principally by one farmer's bad husbandry many more were killed on the Grande Blaye near the Val du Saue. These now seem to have spread to other parts of the island. It is also found in Sark, Herm and Brecqhou, but is probably extinct in Guernsey. The species is now one of the rarest mammals in the British Isles with other colonies only known on remote islands off the Scottish coast and in the Bristol Channel.

Spreading from the East in the 18th Century the **Brown Rat** was also introduced by man into the islands and has become very common on the waste areas and around farm, industrial and domestic buildings. It is frequently seen on beaches. Early 1994 saw a great explosion in their numbers also.

The **House Mouse** is another mammal introduced by human agency and frequently to be found both in country and town areas. The comparatively small amount of corn now grown and stacked in the islands and the small number of poultry kept, has probably contributed to reducing the numbers of both this and the last species. It is generally drab and dull greyish brown.

With a longer tail and generally paler than the house mouse, the **Field-mouse** or **Wood Mouse** also has a white belly to distinguish it. It is quite common. It is certainly an indigenous species. Throughout the Bailiwick the **Long-tailed Field-mouse,** (*Apodemus sylvaticus*) is much larger and more brightly coloured than the British form and is more like the *A. flavicolis*. Its size also varies across the islands, is larger again in Sark and largest of all in Herm. The larger, **Striped Field-mouse,** (*A. agrarius*), was first found by the authors in their garden in Alderney in 1994. Darker, with black tips to the shiny brown hairs, with a pale belly and a pronounced line of dark hairs down its back and along the top of the long tail, it is a very handsome animal.

Also indigenous, the **Bank Vole** is a much sturdier animal than the mouse, with a short stubby tail. It is also quite common, hunts in daylight, but is rarely seen.

The Bailiwick voles, present only in Guernsey and Alderney, are different from those in Jersey, lighter in colour, having short tails and smaller ears. **Field Vole** and **Water Vole** have also been recorded in Guernsey.

The **Shrews** are also different. The little native insectivore *Crocidura russula*, the **Greater White-toothed Shrew,** completely absent from the English mainland, is found in Guernsey, Alderney and Herm. A slightly different species, **The Lesser White-toothed Shrew,** *C. suaveolens,* is found in Jersey, Sark and the Scilly Isles.

Three species of **Bat, Pipistrelle, Long-eared** and **Greater Horseshoe** have been recorded in Guernsey. The first two are common, but the last is probably now extinct. The only species commonly present in Alderney, Sark and Herm is the Pipistrelle, often to be seen at dusk over the wooded parts and in Alderney at Platte Saline, Trois Vaux and Longis Common, frequently hunting insects along the lines of the tarmac roads. Two specimens of Grey Long-eared Bats have been found dead there in the last twenty years and sometimes distinctly larger specimens may be noted in a group flying at dusk, which might possibly be this species.

Herm had a colony of Wallabies, introduced by the tenant, Prince Blücher at the end of the last century which thrived for many years, and Ansted (1862) records documentary evidence of **Red Deer** swimming across from Herm; "up to a very recent time", to land near Vale Castle in Guernsey. We have not seen any other reference to this species being present in historic times.

Not a very impressive list, sixteen or seventeen species in all, present today, for the whole Bailiwick, (not counting the last two), although there may yet be other small species variants to be found by a diligent researcher, but Hirta, one of the islands in the St. Kilda group, half as big again as Alderney, has only one land mammal.

*Chapter 13*

# THE ECOLOGY OF THE BAILIWICK

The number of different habitats for both plant and animal life on any small island is comparatively limited. As has already been noted in the description of the islands and their geology, soil types are limited, there is no chalk, very little clay, only a few marshy areas and few saltmarsh or dune slack areas. Very limited natural pond or still water situations exist. Apart from St. Saviour's Reservoir, the Claire Mare and Vale Pond in Guernsey and Longis and Platte Saline ponds in Alderney, almost all open water areas are in redundant flooded quarries, there are no proper rivers and only a small number of large streams. Many of the smaller streams are not connected directly to the sea, either trickling over the cliffs in short waterfalls, or being absorbed in sand or shingle near the coasts. There are limited areas of woodland, with these generally containing only a small number of tree species.

Despite all these negative factors and the limited indigenous plant and animal life caused by their separation from the continent during the various ice-ages and more recently, each island has a number of species which are peculiar to it, or at least sufficiently rare in other places to excite the interest of naturalists. This is partly due to local climatic conditions, with the islands situated at the northern limit of some Mediterranean species, with infrequent frosts or snow; whilst in some cases they are at the southern limit of more northerly species; and partly to the isolation of some species, for example the White-toothed Shrew, which have not been subject to the genetic changes over the millennia which have affected and modified many plants and animals in large land masses, to help them deal with competition or predation.

The varied types of habitat are frequently small in area and the flora and fauna associated with them limited in numbers. The names of two of the parishes in Guernsey however, Forêt and St. Pierre du Bois, (Forest and St. Peter-in-the-Wood), suggest that these two at least were still heavily wooded in historical times.

Because of their somewhat isolated position and small population, no detailed examination of the flora and fauna of any of the islands was made until the early 18th century, and no worthwhile records appear to have been published before the early 19th. The foundation of the **Guernsey Society of Natural Science and Local Research** in 1882 gave a great impetus to research in both these fields. Monthly lectures were given to members and the subjects discussed recorded, from about 1890, in each year's *Transactions*. Expeditions were made each year to the other islands to investigate various aspects of their history and natural history. This gave rise over the next two or three decades to a wealth of information on the geology, archaeology and natural history of the whole Bailiwick, as well as its folklore and customs. During the years since, much of the research done in all of the islands, by both residents and visiting experts, has continued to be recorded in its pages. The society changed its name to **La Société Guernesiaise** in January 1922.

Three-quarters of a century after the La Société was founded, the formation of the **Alderney Society** in 1966, to create and manage the Museum, soon gave rise to the formation of a Natural History Group under the chairmanship of Vic Mendham, a retired biology teacher who had been coming to the island with school groups to examine its wildlife, for a number of years, before settling here. His wide ranging interest in a number of branches of biological sciences helped to create a series of records of plants, birds, insects, marine life, etc., from the late 1950s, which were continued by his widow almost to the present day. Although never large in numbers, the group has always managed to maintain a few active members and provides a focus for visiting naturalists to report their finds. Although the Society has its own *Bulletin,* (produced until 1989 on a duplicator), many of the records and reports are also published in Guernsey, in *Transactions,* which is well respected and naturally has a much wider circulation.

In updating the checklist of the island's flora, between 1986 and 1988, (which had not been seriously studied for almost a century, since Marquand spent about three years here at the end of the 19th century), the present authors noted about 80 species of plants which had not previously been recorded. It is highly unlikely that more than a handful of these were new to the island within the previous decade or so and far more likely that they had been overlooked previously, by botanists who had simply not been here at the right time of year, or who had perhaps not bothered to report or publish their finds, not realising that many plants common in England are rare or normally absent here. About 20 more species have been added since 1988. Most of the new plant finds in the Bailiwick are also recorded each year, either in *Watsonia,* the technical publication of the BSBI, or in the Society's thrice-annual News.

The formation of **La Société Serquiaise** in 1974 intensified effort in similar research in that island, and their findings also appear in *Transactions.* Since 1980 this society has been affiliated to **La Société Guernesiaise** and has a representative on its Council. Like the others it has a number of special interest sections, with records of plants, birds, insects, mammals etc. seen, being kept regularly.

Bird records in Alderney and Sark have been greatly improved by the annual activities of the Channel Island sea-bird count, the bird-ringers from Guernsey and Jersey and the intermittent presence over many years of Peter Conder, a former President of the RSPB, who maintained a flat at Fort Essex in Alderney for a long period, until his death in 1993. A number of residents in the smaller islands are keen amateur bird-watchers and regularly report their sightings to the groups.

The several unique or rare species of wildlife present on all of the islands, attracts visiting naturalists, both as individuals and organised groups, mainly in the past from Britain, but with increasing numbers coming from European countries, Canada and the U.S.A. in recent years. Some of these visitors too make contributions to the records of species encountered. The geological formations and archæological remains also attract many whose interests lie in those fields.

In recent years much interest has developed amongst the general population, in wildlife programmes on TV and an excellent series of programmes was made about Jersey flora and fauna for Channel TV. The Tourist Board in Guernsey also commissioned video tapes of the islands and in 1994 and 1995, huge numbers of these were sent out free to potential holiday makers in Britain and Europe to encourage tourists. They included a number of shots of interesting wildlife in Guernsey, Alderney and Sark. The authors have encouraged a number of visiting TV teams to include various aspects of the Alderney wildlife in their programmes and assisted in their production. We have each contributed a number of articles to local magazines and journals, including an illustrated series on Alderney wildlife to the Aurigny Airlines twice yearly in-flight magazine, *En Voyage*, which have helped in some small way to raise the awareness of the fragile nature of the environment and the interesting things to be seen by those who take the trouble to look.

Several sets of Guernsey stamps have been issued depicting that island's wildlife, including a set of four Guernsey Marine Life stamps issued, in October 1990 in conjunction with the World Wide Fund for Nature (WWF), formerly the World Wildlife Fund, whilst a similar set of four Alderney stamps was issued in November 1993 depicting a range of the marine organisms found locally. More recently, Brian has supplied photographs of some of the island's more interesting plants, birds, other animals and insects for the production of the present series of Alderney 'Definitive' postage stamps, first issued in May 1994.

Guernsey is well cultivated, with a large dairy industry and well established horticultural production. The large areas of glass, highly visible to all approaching the island by air, formerly concentrated mainly on tomato and fruit production, but are now given over in many cases to commercial flower crops for the English markets.

The ecology of the smaller islands especially is very susceptible to the effect of the frequent strong salt-laden winds, which, although predominantly South-westerly, come from a variety of directions and many of our plants are restricted in size both by these and by the activities of the large rabbit populations. Species which cannot tolerate these conditions do not survive for long, an obvious factor in the reduced number of species compared with the larger islands and the mainlands, both of UK and Europe. Tree seedlings also do not survive grazing by the rabbits, and natural regeneration of these is often minimal. The lack of any major source of water other than local rainfall is also a dominant factor in determining the number and type of species which are present.

In Sark about 50% of the island is under arable cultivation and in Herm much of the plateau land, despite its very thin soil, is either managed grassland to feed the dairy herd, or cultivated to produce local vegetables. In Alderney on the other hand, the decline of agriculture since the 1960s, when the market garden enterprise failed and the changing habits of the population has had a marked effect on the island's ecology and for that matter its economy. Only a small part of the land on the Blayes is now regularly cultivated. Apart from small quantities for animal feed, no cereals are grown, some potatoes are grown and there is a small market garden enterprise run in Le Vallée by a local greengrocer but, apart from individual domestic production, nearly all other vegetables are imported. There is far more permanent grassland, some of which is rarely grazed, or mown for hay and, because furze is no longer cut as a fuel for ovens and fires, scrub has encroached. This has resulted in a tremendous spread of bracken and bramble, in the last thirty to forty years, especially over the cliff areas which were once common land. The cessation of the custom of the winter banon means that cattle no longer roam the Blayes freely in the winter, to help clean up the uncut parts and manure the land, vraic is little used now to fertilise the fields, producing a marked effect on the soil structure and water-retaining properties of the soil and the artificial fertilisers used instead, which add nothing to soil structure, are helping to pollute the water supplies.

There is also an increasing and regrettable usage of herbicides for controlling bracken, bramble, nettles, furze and roadside growth, by both the States and individual landowners, which is affecting small rodent and insect species as well as plants. The provisions of the Mauvaises Herbes Loi, (Noxious Weeds Law) 1933 seem to be no longer enforced, allowing Hogweed, Docks, Thistles, Stinking Onions and Ragwort to spread widely, especially on States' land. Use of insecticides and rodent control by poisons is also affecting the insect and bird populations. The Mauvaises Herbes laws in Guernsey, first introduced in 1927, covering a similar range of plants, are more strictly applied, as is the law of Branquage, requiring landowners and householders to cut back all hedges and vegetation overhanging or obstructing roads and footpaths twice a year, to a required height, at specified periods in June and September. A similar Branquage law exists in the other islands, but in Alderney has not been applied since the 1960s.

The demands of an ever increasing population for housing, water and the disposal of the waste products of the community all have their effect. Sewage in Guernsey and Alderney is currently still pumped out to sea, much of it untreated and in Alderney to no great distance. This will have to stop soon, after the new EEC regulations in 1992 introduced stricter controls. Small communities are supposed to be exempt from these regulations, but local public opinion and the need for clean beaches and water in order to attract tourism, will force the islands into conforming to the specifications.

In Sark where all of the houses are still on cesspits, the sewage is collected and treated at a recently set up central plant at Les Laches. The clear effluent from the filter beds runs through some land and down the cliffs and the powdery solid materials left are recycled on the land.

Alderney has a small treatment centre at the Nunnery which collects the drainage from a part of the town and the effluent passes through the filter beds before mixing with the water from a small stream and flowing across the beach into Longis Bay. The bigger part of the town's drainage runs down to Fort Doyle and, untreated, straight out to sea in a pipe which, at present, finishes far too close inshore. A considerable portion of the island houses have cesspits, which are pumped out regularly and the tanker is emptied here to mix with the drainage from town. Despite this, when the authors organised the local contribution to the Marine Conservation Society's International Beach Clean operation in the autumns of 1993 and 1994, significantly few "sewerage related" items were found on any of the beaches, and Platte Saline Beach, to the west of the outlet, was rated the third cleanest beach in the UK as far as debris on the beach was concerned. It was the only Channel Island Beach in the top twenty in this respect. The schoolchildren now make regular clearances of waste debris from the nearby beach round Braye Bay and for several years the Alderney Rotary Club has made a spring cleanup of the main swimming beaches just before the tourist season starts at Easter.

Guernsey has a considerable number of effluent pipes discharging surface water at various points round the island. The vast majority of the island's foul water is pumped to the macerator at Belle Grêve Bay where it is discharged, otherwise untreated, into the Little Russel channel through a deep-water outfall which was lengthened considerably a few years ago. Many properties in the island have their own cesspits which are emptied regularly and the contents discharged from the tankers into the foul water sewers at a number of points around the island to begin their journey to Belle Grêve.

A comprehensive assessment of the impact on the environment of the disposal of all waste, both solid and foul water is at present underway, at considerable cost.

In due course, when completed, this will be studied and debated by a number of committees and a plan for the long term future of Guernsey's waste devised.

(Jersey already has a system of UV light treatment of the effluent water from their sewage treatment plants which produces probably the cleanest effluent in Europe.)

Disposal of both household and industrial rubbish also presents a huge problem. Whatever plan is eventually agreed upon, which could possibly include the building of a large incinerator plant in Guernsey, the disposal and effects of the final products of the waste disposal system will also be carefully considered.

There old quarries have been used and gradually filled up. Bordeaux Quarry used for many years until it was filled up and landscaped in the last five or six years, is now giving rise to problems in dealing with the methane gas produced by the decaying vegetable materials in the rubbish. Finding an alternative long term site has also proved difficult and costly. Bottle and can collecting points have been established at a number of convenient places round the island.

For generations in Alderney, the rubbish of the island has been tipped over the south cliffs, into the sea at *The Impôt,* after the combustible material has been burnt. Until recently this included all the old builder's waste, paint tins, household equipment, refrigerators, motor cars, etc. In 1990 this was considerably improved and the sea is no longer polluted with the oils, fuels, solvents and propellants from these sources, but the burnt remains of paper, plastic, wood, vegetable refuse, tyres and smaller metal items are still disposed of in this way and dependent on wind direction a nearby area of the cliffs gets spread with unburned or partly burnt paper and plastic and dense, noxious smoke sometimes affects the inland areas. All of the heavier metallic waste is now burnt over, compressed as much as possible and shipped out and sold for scrap in England. Arrangements have been made for all the gases in the refrigerators to be removed to suitable containers first. In 1995, thanks to the activity of the Alderney Shipping Company, a bottle bank was established on the jetty and householders requested to recycle their glass items here. A separate container is provided for metal cans. At the time of writing no arrangements have yet been made to collect empty bottles and cans separately from their biggest producers, the hotels and restaurants. The building of an incinerator at the Impôt has been considered on a number of occasions. About 1992 the cost of this was estimated to be in excess of £250,000, a sum outside the reach of the small community, already suffering from increasing costs of all the services provided and decreasing tax income due to a considerable fall in interest rates. There would still have been the problem of atmospheric pollution from the combustion of the rubbish, already a source of concern in those parts of the island affected by smoke drift through the prevailing winds.

Herm and Sark do not have the same problem of disposal of motor vehicles, but their domestic waste is still causing them some concern. In Herm most rubbish is burnt in the Rosière Quarry. At intervals soil is spread over the burnt residues, whilst in Sark bottles and cans are collected from householders for recycling, bundles of newspapers can be left at the Seigneurie, also for recycling. Heavier items such as old refrigerators, washing machines and other appliances are collected separately, at the expense of the householder. These items are all taken to Guernsey for disposal. Individual householders are responsible for composting their own vegetable waste and burning all other rubbish. The refuse left by visitors, in the many waste bins placed about the island, is separated and the combustible material burnt. In the autumn the population, including the children, make a thorough clean up of beaches, paths and roads, to remove any other waste left by the thousands of day visitors in the season.

Pollution in one form or another, including of the beaches and sea and the increasing demands of modern living standards on the water supplies, need to be studied closely in the immediate future if the environment is to be protected. Development proposals, especially for large-scale housing, hotel, or marina projects must be carefully assessed for the ability of the islands to deal with the effect they will have on the environment and the ecology of both land and sea, before any consent is given to implement them and legislation will need to be introduced soon to protect both the environment as a whole and individual aspects of it, such as more effective wildlife and habitat protection laws.

The radiation pollution from the nuclear power station at Flammanville and the Cap de la Hague reprocessing plant, is regularly monitored in shellfish, molluscs and seaweeds from several points in Jersey and Guernsey, in the Race, at Quesnard Point in Alderney, and at the Casquets. Mud or sand from Little Crabby Harbour in Alderney, Bordeaux Harbour in Guernsey and St. Helier Harbour in Jersey is also monitored by the UK MAFF at Lowestoft. Porphyra samples from Quesnard show significantly higher levels of both total ß concentrations and Ruthenium-106 than the samples from Grève de Lecq in Jersey and Fermain Bay in Guernsey over the last 20+ years. Levels rose noticeably in 1975 and have tailed off slowly since, with occasional fluctuations. The annual discharge of Ru-106 from the plant has risen steadily over the same period.

Levels however, are still reputed to be well below the safety margin.

1992 concentrations of Caesium-137 in fish and shellfish were still low and similar to earlier years, giving an estimated exposure dosage through individual average consumption of fish, crustaceans and molluscs, of approximately 1% of the dose limit.

Monitoring of any proposals to extend these facilities and all emissions and movements of radioactive waste by sea are investigated by the island authorities and, where necessary, representations or protests made to the French.

Radon levels in ground water and some of the granite houses on the islands are also checked regularly.

**Conservation in Guernsey.**

After a number of approaches had been made to the States over the years, without much effect, a Conservation Committee was set up by La Société in 1971 under the Chairmanship of Conseiller Eric Bodman. Over the next twenty years or so co-operation between this committee and the States gradually blossomed into today's happy relationship, where La Société is consulted over the management of many areas of public land, and any proposed development in sensitive areas, including the marine environment.

A Conservation Section of La Société was created in the early 1980s and soon attracted many members who keep a careful eye on the environment and give a considerable amount of their time and labour, to voluntary projects to maintain important habitats in both public and private ownership.

The smaller water-filled quarries in Guernsey of which some 25 have been investigated recently and a comprehensive list of plants, insects and birds found in, on and around them, was included in their report. (*The importance of Guernsey Quarries for Conservation* by Gilmour, Thoumine and Vaudin, *Transactions,* 1991, pp92-134).

In 1990 the States initiated the **Environment 2000** project and invited La Société and the National Trust of Guernsey to co-operate in identifying areas for priority land management plans. They had already identified some 35 sites of Nature Conservation Importance, (SNCIs), 13 of which were on land administered by the States, which were then so designated. The States Board of Administration produce a magazine **Environment Today**, first issued in 1992 and available free to the public. These contain articles on the States policy, work done or in hand and information about energy saving in the home and recycling projects.

**Conservation in Alderney.**

The Alderney 'Conservation of the Cliffs and Natural Beauties Law' of 1935, which became the 'Preservation of Natural Beauties and Prevention of Unsightly Buildings Law' in 1936, was repealed in 1957. As a result a scattered rash of buildings, mostly small bungalows, were erected in the 1960's to house the rapidly expanding immigrant population. After a few years, this was brought under some measure of control by the introduction of a State's policy on housing permits and the appointment of a buildings inspector.

After many representations, by several residents over the previous twenty or more years at Chief Pleas sessions, a small start was made, with the introduction in 1990 of an 'Historic Buildings Law' designed to protect the built environment. Eighteen months later a schedule of 'Conservation Areas' was produced where development or alteration to existing buildings was to be limited. Later, specific buildings or archæological sites were placed on its schedules, which gives some degree of protection for man-made structures. Attempts to introduce other protection for natural things, other than the various changes to Green Belt legislation since it was first introduced in 1935, a Bird Protection Ordinance, first passed in 1933, revised in 1949, with several later amendments and a law (rarely, if ever, enforced) forbidding the felling of any tree over 9in. in circumference, without prior planning consent, have met with a complete lack of legislative response from the States over many years of trying, by both individuals including the authors and by various groups.

A small improvement in this situation was created in 1991 when Jon Kay-Mouat, the President of the Alderney States, agreed that the authors should produce an outline of a Wildlife Protection law, in co-operation with the Chairman of the States Agriculture Committee. After several drafts, an enabling law was agreed which would empower the States to protect, by simple Ordinance, any animal or plant species and their habitats, areas of special interest or outstanding natural beauty, including the littoral zone and offshore islands. This was agreed by the Committee and passed to the Procureur in Guernsey early in 1992 to draft the necessary legislation. More than three years later this has still not been received.

Monitoring radon levels from the Alderney granite in the mains water showed a steady drop from 14.83 bequerels per litre in 1987 to 7.72 in 1990, rising again to 16.34 by 1993. The readings are found to be higher when atmospheric pressure is high. (Figures courtesy of the Clerk of the States, David Jenkins).

**Conservation in Sark**

Like Alderney, Sark has no specific wildlife conservation laws but applies the same type of protection for birds as the other islands. There are a number of people with great interest in the flora and fauna of the island, including the Seigneur and his wife, who ensure that rare or special plants and animals are recorded and their habitats not disturbed or endangered unduly by human activity or development proposals.

In such a small, close-knit community this generally presents little difficulty, the several interesting natural features are usually valued by the whole community and, with the existence of the Sark Environmental Group, are in little danger.

**Conservation in Herm**

The activities of the Wood family over the last 45 years have ensured that Herm has been maintained in natural unspoilt conditions. The farmland is carefully cultivated and managed, the cliffs and common have been left in their natural state and footpaths and tracks kept in good order. Tree planting has largely been to replace dead or damaged trees and has been in keeping with the established flora. Such wildlife protection legislation as exists in Guernsey also applies to Herm.

**Erosion**

Coastal erosion is a problem in most of the islands. Although sand dunes have advanced and retreated several times over the millennia, a process which still continues where man has not interfered with the environment, in many cases roads have been built across them close to the sea and sea walls erected to retain the existing land levels. Cliffs also are not immune to the effects of the continuous pounding of the sea, to the effects of landslips after continuous heavy rain or prolonged drought, or even, as has happened in the islands on several occasions, sections have been pulled down, or at least, the soil covering stripped off by the weight of large masses of Hottentot Fig growing on their faces and falling down to the bottom. (A South African plant introduced, probably accidentally, by the Military garrisons in the 19th century, which has thrived in our generally frost-free conditions).

Fortunately, in the Channel Islands most of the cliffs are of hard, granite type rocks or the nearly as hard, Alderney sandstone and the problem is not nearly as acute as in those mainland areas where the cliffs are of chalk or limestone. There are however a number of areas of "Head" in each island where water and frost action over the centuries has crumbled the less hard rocks into layers of sharp edged fragments, many weighing several pounds and the, often thin, layer of soil over and between these gets washed away, especially after prolonged gales have killed the sparse vegetation with the salt deposited on it. These areas are easily distinguished from the rounded, water-worn stones in the raised beaches which, in a several places are visible below the head. After such events it is often several years before the cliff vegetation recovers and prevents further erosion.

The man-made alterations to the natural environment can have a considerable effect on the local flora and fauna. Mobile dunes become fixed, dune slacks no longer receive their regular inundation of salt water, saltmarshes are drained etc. etc. Plants and animals which live in these specialised habitats gradually disappear and some important species are even lost for ever.

Having built the various sea defences to prevent further erosion, to support roads and harbour walls, or prevent flooding of low lying areas, much labour and expense is subsequently incurred in maintaining them. In gale force winds at high spring tides, the sea regularly attempts to restore its former rights and vast quantities of water and seaweed, sometimes with rocks weighing many pounds, are thrown over, to block the roads and flood the adjacent protected land. The walls are breached under the most severe conditions. This is especially noticeable along the west coast in Guernsey and, more rarely, around Braye and Corblets Bays in Alderney. The Alderney Breakwater is a spectacular sight on many occasions every year, when storms raise walls of spray, sometimes up to 60-70m high, along its length and has cost millions over the last 150 years in maintenance and repairing the large breaches made in the wall on a number of occasions. Without the protection of this huge wall erosion of large sections of the dunes around the bay would be commonplace.

In Alderney, the huge German anti-tank wall built round much of Longis Bay, has turned a mobile dune habitat into a fixed one. Some plants which thrive in moving sand have disappeared and been replaced by others which cannot tolerate being buried under layers of sand at frequent intervals. The existence of this wall has also greatly altered drainage from the common behind it. Although under average rainfall conditions the excess water soon drains away through the sandy turf, to the peat below, in periods of prolonged heavy rain flooding occurs. This reached a peak, unknown in living memory, when in the winter of 1994/95, rainfall well above the average over several months, caused water to flood across the road continuously for many weeks and eventually created a single large lake, stretching from the road almost to the Targets.

In Herm, erosion of the common behind the Shell Beach, both by the sea and the pressure of human activity, has been largely stabilised by the planting of Marram Grass, Sand Sedge and other soil-binding plants, contained initially in wire-mesh baskets. These measures have helped to retain and restore the natural moving dune habitat, whilst reducing the excessive wear of the passage of many feet.

To illustrate the natural progression and recession of sand dunes, even in a comparatively short time, the following will serve as an example.

A similar anti-tank wall was built by the Germans to protect Platte Saline, on Alderney's north coast against sea-borne invasion. This was never completed, only the 200-250m at the eastern end from Fort Doyle being finished, but in 1945 when the inhabitants returned to Alderney, along the part in front of the houses formerly at the eastern end, (which the Germans had demolished), the top of the wall, about 1m above road level, was at least 3-4m above the beach. After the houses were rebuilt in 1946/7, their owners used ladders to get down to the beach. Ten years ago the wall was still 1-2m above the dunes created in the interval. Today it is virtually flush, and in times of storm force, dry, N or NW winds, large quantities of fine grit are blown up the dunes onto the road and into the gardens of the houses. The dune area thus created has gradually been stabilised and colonised by many of the plants and animals which can survive in these conditions.

Look along here for Sea Kale, Sea Sandwort, Sea Spurge, Sea Rocket, Sea

Bindweed, Sea Holly, Yellow Horned-poppy, Sea and Sand Couch grasses, Great Quaking Grass, Sand Sedge, Pyramidal Orchid, Hottentot Fig, and several other plants. A large number of invertebrates may be found on or amongst them, including the Sandhill Snail.

By contrast, in Victorian times when the forts were being built, a narrow gauge railway which came round Crabby Bay and through the narrow cutting at the eastern end of this beach, ran along to Clonque on the seaward side of the Platte Saline Battery, beyond the outer wall of this little fort. This wall collapsed onto the beach, (where it remains), in a storm more than twenty years ago. A length of the remaining land on which the railway formerly ran, 5-6m wide, near the junction with the tarmac road, was washed away in a storm in 1989. This left a cliff 2.5-3m high above the beach level at this point, which has gradually filled up again in six years, to a level now less than 1m below the road.

Before the war a natural stone arch existed on the extremity of Tourgis Point about 50m west of here. This had gone by 1945, presumably washed away in a storm, leaving only the lower half of the outer pillar. The line of the railway track inland from this pillar can still be traced as a 1.5-2m wide depression in the grass.

The need to conform to modern accepted standards of waste and sewage disposal, to prevent pollution of the environment on land, of the sea and of the air, will need to be addressed very seriously by the elected authorities in all of the islands in the immediate future. Introduction of comprehensive conservation legislation to protect and preserve the flora and fauna, particularly the several rare or unique species and the many important habitat sites, to enhance those few measures already on our statute books, is also of paramount importance, both for the present and succeeding generations of islanders.

Any resident who reads this book and has concern about any, or all, of these matters is urged to press their States or Chief Pleas representatives to ensure that suitable steps are taken at the earliest possible opportunity to bring this about.

Tourgis Point about 1930

*Chapter 14*

# BAILIWICK WEATHER

The Bailiwick status as a group of small windswept islands means that severe or prolonged frosts and snow, are rare occurrences. The sea temperature rarely falls below 8-10°C and the prevailing winds are from the South-west, off the Atlantic Ocean, having the effect therefore of keeping the air temperature closer to that of the surrounding water. In the period 1951-1980 Guernsey averaged 10 days a year with daytime gales of force 8 (40mph) or over, whilst Alderney averaged 22 days.

Winds from due East, bringing Arctic conditions off the European mainland in winter, or heat-waves in summer, are comparatively rare. In any given year there is a fairly small number of days of little or no wind and extremes of temperature over the small land masses of the islands have generally no time to build up. It is rare for the mid-day temperature at any time to be below freezing in the winter, night frosts are infrequent and when snow does fall it rarely persists for more than two or three days. Conversely, temperatures above 21-23°C only occasionally last for two, or at the most three consecutive days and the highest temperature recorded of 88.6°F (31.4°C) in Guernsey in the extraordinary outburst of heat on 8th September 1911, when the 24 hour mean temperature was 74.6°F (23.7°C), was reflected in Alderney, but the actual temperature reached there was not recorded. Guernsey attained a record 32.8°C (91°F) on 3rd August 1990, beating the previous 1952 record of 31.7°C (89.1°F). The lowest post-war temperature is -7.8°C in January 1963. Comparable Alderney figures are 29.4° in August 1975 and -9.0° on 13th January 1987.

Readily available meteorological records are scanty before 1889 and prehistoric records from peat pollen and geological evidence do little more than confirm that there was no glaciation here during the Ice Ages and that the later vegetation was temperate deciduous forest. The peat beds, situated at around present low-tide level, date from about 4,950 BP, when the sea level was probably some 8-10m below its present level and the sea levels certainly rose again around the islands in late Roman times, around AD 450.

Fogs are another feature of the weather scene. Very low rain cloud sometimes blankets one or more of the islands in winter and sea fog drifting in, in the rare periods of calm air, in both summer and winter, is an occasional feature. This often extends from sea level up to about 100 feet, leaving the upper part of the islands clear. More frequent, especially in summer, is an extensive belt of low fog, sometimes only a few hundred feet thick, moving at speeds up to 30-40 miles an hour, which can envelop the islands and close the airports, for two or even three days at a time. This band of fog often leaves the lower parts of the islands clear, sometimes in bright sunshine and extends from about 150 feet to 5-600 feet, only blanketing the higher part of the islands. Daytime fog at Alderney Airport is consistently at its highest level in July, averaging about 35 hours each year out of 356 hours daylight. The least amount usually occurs in October with 3½ hours out of a possible 325 hours daylight. The records at Guernsey Airport show June and July as the worst months over the 30 year period, each with an average 11 days each year on which fog was recorded. November has the least there, with only 3 days a year on average on which fog was noted. Sark has about 30-35 days a year with significant fog, the worst months being November, January and March.

Annual summaries of Guernsey weather, recorded at a height of about 250 feet, have appeared in *Transactions* since 1889. The first accurate and detailed records of Alderney's weather, are probably those in the Breakwater Engineer's daily logs, which were kept for the whole period of its construction from 1847 to 1871. The last volume of these, Number 9, may be found in the Alderney Museum and covers the period after the construction was finished, from 1st July 1868 to December 31st 1871, some three months after all work on maintenance and repair had finally ceased.

In addition to recording all work done on the breakwater and in the associated quarries, full details are given every day, of wind directions and strength and changes during the day, general weather and sea conditions as observed visually and an accurate record of barometric pressure, corrected in the later records to sea-level, noon temperature, daily rainfall at a height 10 feet above ground, or 48 feet above datum line, tide heights and times and the age of the moon. Monthly and annual summaries are made and the lowest midday temperature recorded in each year from 1852 to 1871 is noted, with the dates on which it occurred, as were the annual extremes of barometric pressure. Duration of sunshine was not recorded.

Since these records were made in the vicinity of Fort Grosnez, the temperatures will probably be marginally less extreme in the highs and lows, than in Town, but there were rarely more than two days together in which the maximum reached more than 21°C, or the minimum remained at zero or below, at noon. The highest recorded in the log-book was 76°F (24°C), on 17th, 18th and 28th July 1868 and the lowest 26°F (-3.3°C) on 15th January 1855 and again on 22nd December 1870. The 1868 Summer was quite exceptional with temperatures of 70° or above, recorded on 9 days in July, (four and three of them consecutive, with a day at 66° between), three days (two consecutive) in August and two (separate) in September. Rainfall recorded showed a maximum of 148.6mm (5.85in) in December 1868 and 150.62mm (5.93in) in December 1869, when the annual total was 805mm (31.69in)

In Jersey annual records of the weather have been published in the *Bulletin* of The Société Jersiaise since about 1880 and from 1906-16 *Transactions* included Alderney's rainfall figures, collected by W.J. Picot, H.M. Procureur, at his house in Le Huret. Here a maximum temperature of 79°F (26.1°C), recorded on 12th August 1914, is one of the few records of temperature made by him. His rainfall figures showed a maximum of 258.6mm (10.18in) in December 1915. Guernsey usually had about 20-25 more hours sunshine than Jersey, at around 2,000 hours per year, some 100 hours more than the south coast of England.

Comparison between the records for Guernsey and Alderney since 1950 show that Alderney generally has about 100 hours less sunshine a year than Guernsey, putting it on a par with the south coast of England and 100-150mm (4-6 inches) less rain. It would seem reasonable to assume that this was also the case a century or more earlier. The early Guernsey records show an average annual rainfall of 34.57in. (878.1mm) over the period from 1894-1913 and 858.9mm average from 1951-1980, whilst Alderney's figures for 1906-13, discounting 1910 where one month was omitted, were 30.61in. (777.5mm) and 768.4mm average from 1957-1976. Sark's from 1905-13, was 28.45in. (722.6mm). These differences between the three islands were fairly consistently maintained, with Sark having less rainfall in total. However, since the Alderney weather station was moved from the high ground in the west of the island, at the Airport (c.240ft) to the low ground at the eastern end by the Lighthouse (c.30ft), the amount of rainfall recorded has decreased by about 100mm and is now about 60mm less than Sark. The amount recorded at the Alderney Breakwater in the 1860s at a height of 48ft was much closer to the present figure. As the prevailing winds are from the SW and rain hits the high ground first, both these figures are understandable. A survey carried out over about a dozen sites in Guernsey from 1907-17, showed a series of bands of total annual rainfall across the island with more falling on the high ground around St. Peter Port, where an average of 36.7in (932.2mm) a year had fallen over the previous 75 years, which was taken as the 100% level, decreasing in stages with 90% at the site where the airport now stands, to the lowest amount (80%) at Claire Mare in the west on the low coast and lower levels all along the west coast to Vale Common (89%) in the low N/NE. The number of wet days in each year is also reasonably consistent, with Guernsey averaging 191 days with measurable rainfall, Sark 175 days and Alderney 160 days. The maximum rainfalls recorded in a year were 56.96in. (1446.8mm) in Guernsey in 1872, 41.94in.

(1065.3mm) in Alderney in 1915 and 1134mm (44.6in.) in Sark in 1994. Jersey has about the same annual rainfall as Alderney, but on an average has about 200 wet days a year.

No detailed weather records for Alderney seem to have survived from the end of the work on the breakwater, except for the 1906-16 records of rainfall, (with a few additional, general comments about storms, frosts etc.), until recording was started again at the airport in 1957. This was continued in a series of Meteorological Office Log Books until August 1979. We traced these books to a storeroom at Guernsey Airport at the time when Jean was Hon. Curator of the Alderney Museum and, through the co-operation of the Chief Meteorological Officer there, they were returned to Alderney in 1988 and are now in the Museum. There was a gap of 26 months from the time these records ceased, until the present daily recording at Alderney Lighthouse was established and since that time the daily records have been sent to the States' offices from there, on a calendar monthly basis.

All records which follow have been converted to mm of rain and degrees Celsius. Sunshine records are in hours, not hours and minutes. The tables were compiled from records kindly supplied by the Met. Office at Guernsey Airport, and the States of Alderney. The Sark records, largely compiled by Mssrs. Hinsley and May were supplied by Roy Cook. (Sark sunshine records only cover July 1989-Dec 1992).

Comparative figures.

## GUERNSEY WEATHER SUMMARY
### Summary for the 10 years 1984-1993

|             | Jan  | Feb  | Mar   | Apr   | May   | June  | July  | Aug   | Sept  | Oct   | Nov   | Dec  | Total   | Av'ge  |
|-------------|------|------|-------|-------|-------|-------|-------|-------|-------|-------|-------|------|---------|--------|
| Temp max    | 11.9 | 11.1 | 13.3  | 17.1  | 21.1  | 23.2  | 24.2  | 25.6  | 22.4  | 18.1  | 15.1  | 13.1 |         | 17.98  |
| Temp min    | -0.4 | -0.8 | 1.1   | 2.2   | 5.7   | 7.7   | 10.3  | 10.5  | 9.4   | 6.4   | 2.8   | 1.3  |         | 4.68   |
| Average max | 8.3  | 7.6  | 9.6   | 11.5  | 14.8  | 16.5  | 19.1  | 19.3  | 17.6  | 14.6  | 11.2  | 9.7  |         | 13.31  |
| Average min | 4.5  | 3.9  | 5.3   | 6.2   | 8.9   | 11.1  | 13.2  | 13.5  | 12.4  | 10.5  | 7.3   | 6.2  |         | 8.58   |
| Average mean| 6.4  | 5.7  | 7.4   | 8.8   | 11.8  | 13.8  | 16.2  | 16.4  | 15.1  | 12.6  | 9.3   | 8.1  |         | 10.94  |
| Rain mm.    | 92.9 | 61.7 | 68.3  | 50.2  | 36.8  | 52.3  | 38.1  | 43.6  | 63.5  | 83.1  | 95.7  | 99.7 | 783.9   | 65.32  |
| Sun hrs.    | 56.8 | 85.2 | 123.1 | 196.1 | 242.7 | 235.4 | 249.1 | 230.1 | 173.3 | 111.9 | 76.4  | 55.3 | 1,835.4 | 152.95 |

## ALDERNEY WEATHER SUMMARY
### Summary for the 10 Years 1984-1993

|             | Jan  | Feb  | Mar   | Apr   | May   | June  | July  | Aug   | Sept  | Oct   | Nov   | Dec  | Total   | Av'ge |
|-------------|------|------|-------|-------|-------|-------|-------|-------|-------|-------|-------|------|---------|-------|
| Temp max    | 12.7 | 11.8 | 13.1  | 15.6  | 18.2  | 20.3  | 21.6  | 23.1  | 21.9  | 18.8  | 16.1  | 14.7 |         | 17.3  |
| Temp min    | 0.5  | 0.6  | 1.8   | 3.1   | 6.2   | 8.1   | 10.2  | 10.5  | 10.1  | 7.6   | 3.6   | 1.8  |         | 5.3   |
| Average max | 9.3  | 8.4  | 10.1  | 11.7  | 14.3  | 16.5  | 18.6  | 19.2  | 18.1  | 15.3  | 12.6  | 10.8 |         | 13.7  |
| Average min | 5.6  | 4.8  | 6.1   | 6.8   | 9.1   | 11.2  | 13.6  | 13.9  | 13.3  | 11.2  | 8.2   | 6.9  |         | 9.2   |
| Average mean| 7.5  | 6.6  | 8.1   | 9.2   | 11.7  | 13.8  | 16.1  | 16.6  | 15.7  | 13.3  | 10.4  | 8.9  |         | 11.4  |
| Rain mm.    | 83.1 | 42.7 | 50.7  | 48.8  | 29.6  | 44.7  | 41.1  | 35.9  | 51.2  | 77.7  | 68.1  | 88.5 | 662.1   | 55.2  |
| Sun hrs.    | 52.9 | 83.2 | 124.1 | 189.1 | 238.6 | 224.3 | 238.3 | 225.7 | 168.4 | 104.9 | 76.5  | 52.2 | 1,778.2 | 148.2 |

## SARK WEATHER SUMMARY
### Summary for the 10 Years 1984-1993

|             | Jan  | Feb  | Mar   | Apr   | May   | June  | July  | Aug   | Sept  | Oct   | Nov   | Dec  | Total  | Av'ge |
|-------------|------|------|-------|-------|-------|-------|-------|-------|-------|-------|-------|------|--------|-------|
| Temp max    | 11.9 | 12.1 | 14.3  | 17.6  | 20.9  | 23.9  | 25.7  | 26.9  | 20.9  | 20.2  | 16    | 13.7 |        | 18.7  |
| Temp min    | -0.4 | -0.6 | 0.3   | 2.2   | 5.3   | 7.6   | 10.1  | 10    | 7     | 5.5   | 2.4   | 1.1  |        | 4.2   |
| Average max | 8.5  | 8.6  | 10.4  | 11.2  | 15.7  | 17.2  | 20    | 20.5  | 16.6  | 15.5  | 11.6  | 10   |        | 13.8  |
| Average min | 4.4  | 3.8  | 5.5   | 6.4   | 8.8   | 10.8  | 13.2  | 13.8  | 11.3  | 11    | 7.9   | 6.3  |        | 8.6   |
| Average mean| 6.5  | 6.2  | 7.9   | 8.8   | 12.2  | 14    | 16.6  | 17.2  | 14    | 13.2  | 9.7   | 8.1  |        | 11.2  |
| Rain mm.    | 89.9 | 53.3 | 60.6  | 47.9  | 34.6  | 48.5  | 36.8  | 40.1  | 60    | 86.5  | 89.7  | 97.6 | 745.4  | 62.1  |
| Sun hrs.    | 86.2 | 71.4 | 119.1 | 162.8 | 147.8 | 137.6 | 220.6 | 228.3 | 143.8 | 90.6  | 66.4  | 57.6 | 1,532  | 127.7 |

# SELECTED BIBLIOGRAPHY

| | | |
|---|---|---|
| Allen, Ann | Field Companion to the Flowers of Sark | 1993 |
| | Sark; Invertebrates of the Rocky Shore | 1989 |
| | Gouliot Caves (Sark) | 1988 |
| Anstead, D.T. & Latham, R.G. | The Channel Islands | 1862 |
| Babington, C.C. | Primitiae Florae Sarnicae | 1839 |
| Belle, Dr. A. | Dragonflies of Alderney | 1980 |
| Berry, W. | A History of the Island of Guernsey | 1815 |
| Bichard, J. & McClintock, D. | Wild Flowers of the Channel Islands | 1975 |
| Bonnard, B. | Flora of Alderney | 1988 |
| | Channel Island Plant Lore | 1993 |
| | Out and About in Alderney | 1995 |
| Briggs, P.M. | Discover Wild flowers in the Channel Islands | 1992 |
| Cochrane, Jennifer | Life on Sark; through the year | 1994 |
| Coysh, Victor | The Visitor's Guide to Guernsey, Alderney & Sark | 1989 |
| | Alderney. (2nd Ed.) | 1989 |
| de Pomerai, N & Robinson, R. | The Rocks and Scenery of Guernsey | 1994 |
| Dobson, R. | Birds of the Channel Islands | 1952 |
| Freeman, R.B. | Fauna of Alderney | 1980 |
| Gibbons, W. | The Rocks of Sark | 1975 |
| Hawkes, K. | Sark | 1977 |
| Hill, Mike G. | The distribution of breeding Seabirds in the Bailiwick of Guernsey; 1986-1990 | 1991 |
| | Seabirds of the Bailiwick of Guernsey 1986-92 | 1993 |
| Jee, N. | Guernsey's Natural History | 1967 |
| Kendrick, Jill S. | Fifty Sea Shells from Herm Island | 1969 |
| Kendrick, T. | Archaeology of the Channel Islands Vol. 1. The Bailiwick of Guernsey | 1928 |
| Lukis, F.C. | Collectanea Antiqua. (6 MS volumes) | 1853 |
| McClintock, D. | The Wild Flowers of Guernsey | 1974 |
| | Joshua Gosselin; Botanist & Antiquary | 1976 |
| | Guernsey's Earliest Flora | 1984 |
| | Wild Flowers of Guernsey. (Supplement) | 1987 |
| Marquand, E.D. | Flora of Guernsey & the Lesser Channel Islands | 1901 |
| | Supplement to Flora T.S.G. | 1921 |
| Mendham, M.L. | A List of the Birds of Alderney | 1990 |
| Renouf, J. & Urry, J. | The First Farmers in The Channel Islands | 1976 |

| | | |
|---|---|---|
| Roach, Topley, Brown, Bland and D' Lemos Rountree, F.R.G. | An outline and Guide to the Geology of Guernsey | 1991 |
| | Birds of Sark | 1974 |
| | Supplement to the Birds of Sark | 1991 |
| Société Guernesiaise, La | Transactions (Annually) | 1882-1994 |
| | Wildflowers of the Bailiwick of Guernsey (Edited by G. Caldwell) | 1994 |
| | Rocks and Scenery of Guernsey | 1991 |
| Toms, Carel | Country Walks by the Sea in Guernsey 5 booklets | 1967-91 |
| Wood, J | Herm, Our Island Home | 1972 |

There are many entries concerning the flora, fauna, geology, ecology and archaeology of the Bailiwick, in the 112 years of annual publications of *Transactions* of La Société Guernesiaise, too numerous to mention here. The annual reports of the various specific interest "Sections" of the Society also furnish a wealth of detail on new species of plants and animals found in the previous year. A full set of copies of this publication can be consulted in the Guille-Allès Library, the Priaulx Library and at the HQ of La Société Guernesiaise at Candie Gardens, in Guernsey and at the Alderney Library and the Alderney Society Museum in Alderney.

The reader is also referred to the *Bulletin* of the Alderney Society, published since its formation in 1966, at first quarterly and now, since 1989, annually. These are also available for consultation at the Alderney Library and the Alderney Society Museum.

La Société Serquiaise was founded in 1975 and issues an annual newsletter, primarily for its many off-island members. As noted in the Introduction it was affiliated with La Société Guernesiaise in 1984. Most of the reports on the island's flora, fauna and history, written since 1882 have appeared in *Transactions*.

Further relevant references will be found in the *Bulletin* of La Société Jersiaise, published annually since its foundation in 1876.

Most of the books mentioned above, published after 1975 will be found on sale in the bookshops or Museums in one or other of the islands.

There are also many histories of, and guide books to, the Channel Islands or to the Bailiwick of Guernsey alone, which have been published in the last 250 years which contain brief references to the natural history of the area. Only a few of the more important have been included in the list above. Most of these are available for consultation at the two libraries in Guernsey. A few are also available at the Alderney Library.

# Index

Note; Latin names of species shown in italics. Figures in bold type indicate an illustration

## A

*Actinia*, 76
Adder's-tongue, Common, 17, 65
    Least, 17, 65, **86**
    Small, 17, 65
Adonis Pool, 24
*Agaricus*, 60
*Aiptasia*, 76
Airport, Alderney, 23
    Guernsey, 16
*Alaria*, 57
Albecq Bay, 17
Alderney, 55
Alderney Sandstone, 9
    Agricultural Society, 127
    Cow, 127
    Geranium, 66
    granite, 9
    Hoard, 32
    Lighthouse, 21
    Sea Lavender, 66, **83**
    Shipping Company, 137
    Society, The, iii, 121, 133
    Society Museum, iii, 32, 63, 121, 133, 145
*Aleuria*, 62
Alexanders, 67
Algae, Freshwater, 58
    Marine, 55
*Allium*, 70
Allseed, Four-leaved, 67
Alluvium, 7
Amfroques, Les, **93**, 123
Ammonite, 28
*Amoeba*, 103
*Amphipholis*, 78
*Anaboena*, 59
*Andrena*, 118
Andros, Thomas, ii
Anemone, Beadlet, **46**
    Snakelocks, 98

Anstead, D.T., vi
*Anthopleura*, 76
*Anthropora*, 118
Ants, 118
Aphids, 119
*Aplexa*, 105
Aplite, 9
Aquatic Mammals, 102
*Argyroneta*, 105
Arsenal, 130
Arthropods, 120
Artichoke, Globe, 69
*Arum*, 71
Ascidia, 75
Ascidians, **47**, 75
*Ascidiella*, 75
Asparagus, Wild, 70
*Atrichum*, 64
Augustinian Priory, Herm, 30
Aurigny Airlines, 134
Autelets, Les, (Sark), 25
Autumn Lady' Tresses, 72, **91**
*Azolla*, 65

## B

Babington, C.C., iii, vi, viii
Backswimmer, 104
Badger, x
*Balanoglossus*, 77
*Balanus*, 79
Banon, 135
Barnacle, 79
    Acorn, **37**, 79
    Darwin, 79
    Goose, **36**, 79, **107**
*Bartramia*, 63
Bats, 131
Bedstraw, Ladies, **89**
Bee, 112
    Bumble, 118
    Cuckoo, 118
    flower, 118
    hive, 118
    honey, 118
    leaf-cutter, 118

    mining, 118
    Solitary, 118
Beetle, Bloody-nosed, 120
    Carnivorous Water, 104
    Cockchafer, **39**, 119
    Devil's Coach Horse, 119
    Great Diving, 104
    Lesser Stag, 120
    Minotaur, 120
    Oil, 120
    Rose Chafer, 119
    Sexton, 119
    Silver Water, 104
    Tortoise, 119
    Violet Ground, 119
    Whirligig, 104
Belemnite, 28
Bell-shaped Mottlegill, **41**, 61
Belle Gréve Bay, 18
Belvoir Bay, 26, 27
Bermuda Grass, 71, **91**
Bibette Head, **33**
*Bifurcaria*, 57
Bindweed, Black, 69
    Sea, 143
Bird's-foot, 67, **82**
    Orange, 67, **82**
Birds, lists of, 121
Black Bulgar, 62
Blackbird, 124
Bladder Weed, 57
Blanket Weed, 59
Blenny, Butterfly, 101
    Montague's, 100
Blenny, Tompot, 101
Bluebell, **88**
Blue-green algae, 59
Blue Bridge, 22
Bluestone Bay, 9
*Boletus*, 60
*Bombus*, 118
Bonne Terre, Le Val de la, 19, 106
Bordeaux Quarry, 137
*Botrylloides*, 76
*Botryllus*, 76

*Bovista,* 60
Brachiopod, 28
Bracken, 65
Branquage, Law of, 135
Braye Bay, 21
    Common, 9
Braye du Valle, 15
Breadcrumb Sponges, **46**, 75, 98
Breakwater, 21
    Journal, 145
Bream, 106
Brecqhou, 12, 24, 25, 55, 113, 130
Bristle-tail, 79
British Red Data Book, 66
Brittle-stars, 78
Brome, Rescue, 71
*Bromus,* 71
Bronze Age, 32, 53
Broom, Prostrate, 68, **90**
Broomrape, x, 68
    Carrot, 68
    Common, 68
    Greater, 68
    Ivy, 68
    Purple, 68
Bryophytes, 63
*Buccinum,* 98
Bullfinch, 124
Bunting, Cirl, 122
*Bupleurum,* 67
Burhou, viii, ix, 1, 9, 19, **33**, 123, 129
Burnet Rose, 27, **89**
Butcher's Broom, 27
Butterbur, 72
    Giant, 72, **87**
Butterfish, 101
Butterflies, list of common, 113
    photos, **39**
Butterfly, Glanville Fritillary, xi
Buzzard, 126

# C
Cabou, 100
Cachalière, 9
*Calliergonella,* 64

*Caloplaca,* 62
*Calvatia,* 60
*Campylopus,* 64
Canary Grass, 71
Cap de la Hague, 1, 5, 18, 50
    Atomic reprocessing plant, 138
Carp, 106
    Grass, 106
    Wild, 106
Carrageen, 57
Casquets, viii, ix, 1, 19, 123, 138
Castle Cornet, 7
Catworm, 77
Cauliflower Fungus, 61
Centipedes, 120
Ceratodon, 64
Chaffinch, 124
Chalk, ix
Chanterelle, 61
Chapel of St. Tugual, 27
Charles the Simple, 49
Charophytes, 60
Château de Marais, 7
Chausey Isles, 1
Chief Pleas, Sark, 24
Chiff-chaff, 124
Chinaman's Cap, 98
*Chironomus,* 104
Chiton, 97
*Chlamydomonas,* 59
*Chlorella,* 60, 103
Chlorophyceae, 59
*Chondrostereum,* 62
*Chroolepus,* 59
*Chthamalus,* 79
Chub, 106
*Cladonia,* 63
*Cladophora,* 57, 59
Clams, 99
Clare Mare, 17, 122
*Clavelina,* 75
*Clavulinopsis,* 62
Clay, 9, 13
*Clitocybe,* 60, 61
Clonque, 143
    Bay, 22

Clouded Agaric, 61
Clover, Atlantic, 68
    Western, 68
    White, 68
Clubmoss, Mossy, 65
Cobo, 7
    Bay, 17
Cobo granite, 17
Cock's-eggs, 73
Cockroaches, **111**, 119
*Codium,* 57
*Colletes,* 118
Colonial Animals, 75
*Coloplaca,* 63
Comfrey, ii
Common Earthball, 61
Common Tern, 123
Conehead, Long-winged, 117
Conservation Areas, 140
Conservation of the Cliffs and Natural Beauties Law, 139
*Convoluta,* 77
Coot, 125
Copper, 13
*Coprinus,* 60
Coque Lihou, 123
*Corallina,* 56, 78
Corals, 28, 77
Corals, Soft, 77
Corblets Bay, 142
    Quarry, 9, 65, 106, 117
*Cordyline,* 71
Cormorant, 122
Corvée, feudal custom, 24
*Corynactis,* 77
Cott, 59
Cotton Spinner, 78
Coupée, La, 24
Cowrie, European, 97
Crab, Chancre, 80
    Edible, 80
    Fiddler, 80
    Hairy, 80
    Hermit, 80
    Lady, 80

Porcelain, 80
Shore, 80
Spider, 80
Velvet Swimming, 80
Crabby Bay, 66, 143
Crane's-bill, Pencilled, **87**
*Crassostrea,* 99
Crayfish, 80
Creux Belet, 25
Creux Derrible, 24
Creux des Fées, 16
Creux ès Faies, Le, 29
Creux Harbour, 23
Crevichon, 27, 55, 65
Cricket, Great Green Bush-, **111**, 117
    Grey Bush, 117
    House, 118
    Speckled Bush, 117
Crickets, 117
Crinum, 70
*Crocidura,* 131
Crocus, Sand, 70, **89**
Cromlechs, 30
Crustacea, 79
Cuckoo, 125
Cudweed, Cape, 69
    Jersey, 69
Cushion Star, 78
Cuttlefish, 98
Cyanophyceae, 59
*Cynara,* 69
Cypress, Monterey, 66
*Cytisus,* 68

# D

Dab, 100
Dabberlocks, 57
*Dacrymyces,* **42**, 62
Daisy, St. Peter Port, 69
Damselflies, 117
    list of, 117
Dartford Warbler, xi, 124
de Carteret, Helier, 51
Dead Man's Fingers, **40**, **45**, 60, 77

Deer, 127
Déhus, Le, 29
Derrible Bay, 24
*Desmarestia,* 58
Desmids, 60
Diatoms, 60
*Dicranella,* 64
*Dicranum,* 64
*Dictyota,* 57
*Diodora,* 97
Diorite, 7, 9
    orbicular, 9
*Diplodontus,* 105
Diver, 123
Dixcart Bay, 25
Dog-whelk, **37**, 98
    Netted, 98
Dolerite, 9
Dolmen, Robert's Cross, Herm, **52**
Dolphin, Bottlenosed, 102
    Common, 102
Doüit, 20
Dove, Collared, 124
    Rock, 124
    Stock, 124
    Turtle, 124
Dragonflies, 116
    list of, 117
Dragonfly nymphs, 104
*Drepanocladus,* 64
Druce, G.C., ix
Druids, 32
Duck, Mandarin, 126
    Tufted, 124
Duckweed, Ivy-leaved, 71
    Least, 71
Duke of Argyll's Tea Tree, 73
Dulse, 57, 98
Duncan, J, vi
Dunnock, 124, 125
Dupuy, Edgar, v
Dwarf Millet, 71

# E

Eagle, White-tailed, 123
Early Sand-grass, 71

Earth Star, Common, 61
Earwigs, 119
Echinoids, 28
Echium, Giant, 73
Ecology, 132
Ecrehous, 1
Eel, 106
Eel-grass, 16
Elder, 61
*Eleaeagnus,* 73
Elephant's Tusk, 98
Elizabeth I, 51
Elm, Female, 74
    Hybrid Guernsey, 74
    Male, 74
    White, 74
    Wych, 74
*Elminius,* 79
Elvers, 106
*Enteromorpha,* 56, 57, 58
Environment 2000 project, 139
Epérquerie, Sark, 25
*Erigeron,* 69
*Escallonia,* 73
Essex Castle, 22
Essex Hill, 31, 65, 129
Etac de la Quoire, 9
Étacs, Les, 123
*Eudorina,* 59
*Euglena,* 59, 103
*Eupagurus,* 80

# F

Fairy Grotto, 25
Fan Worm, 77
Farm animals, 127
Fauna, 53
Fauxquets Valley, 18
Feather Star, 78
Felsite, 12
Felspar, 9
Fermain Bay, 16
Fern, Buckler, 65
    Golden-scaled Male, 65
    Guernsey, 65
    Hart's-tongue, 65

Jackson's, 65
Jersey, 65
Lady, 65
Male, 65
Royal, 65
Rusty-back, 65, **86**
Water, 65
Field-mouse, 131
Field Blewit, 60
Field Maple, 74
Fieldfare, 125
Fish, 99
Fish Factory, the old, 17
Fissidens, 64
Flammanville, Atomic Energy Power Station, 138
Flatworms, 103
Flies, 119
Flint tools, 29
Flora, 53
Flowering plants, 66
Fluellen, Sharp-leaved, 69
Fontaine David, La, 21
Forest, (Parish), 132
Fort Albert, 21
  Clonque, 22, **96**
  Essex, 22, 133
  Grey, 16
  Hommeaux Florains, 123
  Hommet, 17
  Isle de Raz, 22
  Le Crocq, 17
  Le Marchant, 18
  Pezeries, 16
  Quesnard, 65
  Richmond, 17
  Sausmarez, 16
  Tourgis, 19, 23, 30
Fossils, 28
Fouillages, Les, 29
Fox, x
*Fragaria*, 72
Frairies, 50
Franks, 49
Frog, Common, 108
  Jersey Agile, 108

Froghoppers, 119
Fuchsia, Hedge, 73
Fulmar, 122, 123
*Fumaria*, 64, 67
Fumitory, Boreau's, 67
*Furcellaria*, 57

## G

Gabbro, 7, 9
Galeux, 123
Gall-wasp, 119
*Gammarus*, 104
Gannet, xi, 121, 122
Garden Rocks, 22, 123
Gardiens, Les, 22
Garfish, 101
Garnesee Violets, ii, 68
Geese, Brent, 123
Geranium, 66
Gerarde, 80
*Gibbula*, 97
Giffoine, Le, 22, 123
*Gigartina*, 57
Glasswort, Prostrate, 72
*Glyceria*, 105
*Gnaphalium*, 69
Gnat, 104
Gneiss, quartz-biotite, 12
Goat, Golden Guernsey, 127
Goby, 2-spotted, 101
  Rock, 100
  Sand, 100, 101
Godin, 123
Godwit, Bar-tailed, 121
Golden Orfe, 106
Goldfinch, 124
Goldfish, 106
*Golfingia*, 77
Goose, Brent, 121
Goose-foot Star, 78
*Gordius*, 103
Gorse, 62
Gosselin, Joshua, v, viii, 30, 110
Gouliot Caves, 12, 24, 25
Grand Havre, 17
  Blaye, 23
  Grève, 24

Grande Mare, La, 17, 122
Granite, 9
Granite, Bibette Head, 9
  red Cobo type, 7
  augen-gneiss, 7
Granodiorite, 7, 12
Granodiorite gneiss, 7
Grass, Bermuda, 71
  Canary, 71
  Hare's-tail, 71
  Yellow Bristle, 71
Grasshopper, Blue-winged, 118
  Common Field, 118
  Meadow, 118
Grasshoppers, 117
Great Quaking Grass, 143
Great Russel, 15
Grebe, 123
Green Belt, 140
Green Leaf Worm, 77
Greenfinch, 124
Grey Partridge, 126
Guernsey cattle, 18, 54, **93**, **94**
Guernsey Cow, 127
Guernsey Lily, ii
Guernsey Museum and Art Gallery, vi, 30, 32
Guernsey Lily, ii
Guernsey Society of Natural Science and Local Research, The, iii, vii, 132
Guet, Le, 17
Guillemot, 123
Gull, Black-headed, 123
  Great Black-backed, 123
  Herring, 122, 123
  Lesser Black-backed, **92**, 123

## H

Hair Mosses, 64
Hairworms, 103
*Halichondria*, 75
*Haliotis*, 98
*Hallictus*, 118
Hanging Rocks, 63

Hannaine Bay, 22, 123
Hanois Lighthouse, 15
Hare, x, 129
Hare's-ear, Small, 67, **82**
Harrier, Hen, 126
    Marsh, 126
Harvestmen, 120
Havre Gosselin, 24
Hawfinch, 124
Head, 7, 9, 141
Hebe, 73
Hedgehog, x, **34**, 129
    Blond, x, **34**, 129
*Hellebore,* ii
Hemiptera, 104
Hemp Agrimony, 72
Henry VIII, 50
Herbivores, 128
Herm, xii, 1, 30, 55, 77
    Manoir, 27
    mine, 26
    obelisk, 27
    Oysters, 99
Heron, Grey, 125
    Purple, 125
*Himanthalia,* **48**
Historic Buildings Law 1990, 140
Hobby, 126
Hog's Back, Sark, 24
Hogweed, 135
Holly, New Zealand, 73
Holy Islands, 31
Hommeaux Florains, Les, 21
Honey Fungus, 60
Hoopoe, 125
Hornblende, 12
Horned-poppy, Yellow, 58
Hornet, 118
Horsetail, 65
    Great, 65, **81**
    Water, 65
Hottentot Fig, 55, 141, 143
Hound's-tongue, 69
House Sparrow, 125
Hoverflies, 118, 119
Huguettes, Les, 32, 53

Humps, The, 123
Hurd Deep, 2, 5
*Hydra,* 103
*Hydrarachna,* 105
*Hydrobia,* 105
*Hydroides,* 78
Hydroids, 76
*Hygrocybe,* 62
Hymenoptera, 112
*Hypericum,* 67
*Hypnum,* 64

# I

Ice Age, ix, 1
Ice Age, Great, 2
Impôt, The, 137
Ink-cap, Common, 61
Insects, 112
Irish Moss, 57
Iron Age, 32, 53
Island Hall, 20

# J

Jackdaw, 124
Jay, 124
Jellyfish, Common, 76
    Compass, 76
    Octopus, 76
    Portuguese Man-of-War, 76
    Stalked, 76
Jerbourg peninsula, 7
Jersey, 55
Jersey cattle, 54
Jethou, 1, 27, 30, 55, 113
Jew's-Ear Fungus, **42**, 61
Jewel Anemones, 77
Jewel Caves, 24
*Juncus,* 70

# K

Kestrel, 126
King's Mills, 65
King Alfred, 49
Kingfisher, 126
Kittiwake, 123

# L

L'Ancresse Common, 18, 29, 65
L'Emauve, 30
L'Erée, 16, 122
    Bay, 17
L'Essource, 19
L'Etac de la Quoire, 123
Ladybirds, 119
Ladysmith, 20
*Laminaria,* 57
*Lampranthus,* **88**
Lamprophyte, 9
Lancresse Common, 7
Land's End, 16
*Langermannia,* 60
Langlois, L.J.A., 129
Language, 50
*Lassea,* 56
Latham, R.G., vi
*Lathyrus,* 72
Lavender, ii
Laver, 56
Lavoiret, 20
Le Fort, Sark, 25
Lead, 12
Leafhoppers, 119
*Leathesia,* 58
*Lecanora,* 62
Leech, Horse, 104
Leek, Three-cornered, 70
Leland, John, 53
*Lepas,* 79
*Lepidochitona,* 97
*Lepidopleurus,* 97
*Lepiota,* 60
*Lepista,* 60
Les Boutiques, 25
Les Laches, (Sark), 136
Les Porciaux, 30
*Lichena,* 63
Lichens, **43**, 56, 62
*Lichina,* 56
Lighthouse, Alderney, 21
    Hanois, 15, **95**
    Point Robert, 25
Lihou Island, 16, 29, 55, 72

Lily, African, 70
    Cuban, 70
    Guernsey, 70
    Jersey, 70
*Limonium,* 66
Limpet, Blue-rayed, 97
    Common, 97
    Keyhole, 97
    River, 105
Linnet, 122, 124
*Lithophyllum,* 57
*Lithothamnion,* 57
Little Auk, 123
Little Burhou, 19
Little Crabby Harbour, 138
Little Russel Channel, 15, 26
Little Sark, 12, 24, 30
*Littorina,* 97
Lizard, Green, 108
Lobster, Edible, 80
    Squat, 80
Loess, 7, 12
*Lomentaria,* 57
Longis Bay, 22, 117, 142
Longis Common, 9, 30, 32, 107, 131
Longis Pond, ix, 22, 59, 108, 117, 125, 132
Lords and Ladies, 71
    Large, 71
Luff, W.A., 112
Lugworm, 77
Lukis, F.C., vi, 30, 110
Lukis family, 30
*Lycoperdon,* 60

# M
MacCulloch, Dr. J, v
Magpie, 124
Mallard, 126
Mannez Garenne, 129
Mannez Pond, 65, 106, 108, **109**, 117, 125
Mannez Quarry, 106
Manx Shearwater, 121
*Marchantia,* **44**

Marine Conservation Society, 98
Marigold, Corn, x
Marine worms, 77
Marjoram, ii
Marquand, vi, 55, 58, 66, 110, 133
Marram Grass, 58, 142
Martello towers, 18
Martin, House, 124
    Sand, 124
Mary I, 51
Masseline Harbour, 24
Mauvaises Herbes Loi, ix, 135
May-bug, 119
McClintock, D., v
Medick, Black, 68
Megalithic Culture, 31
    graves, 31
    monuments, 13
    passage graves, 29
*Melanoleuca,* 61
*Membranipora,* 77
Mendham, M.L., 121
    Vic, 108, 133
Mericarp, 106
Merlin, 126
Mermaid Tavern, Herm, 27
Mesozoa, 103
*Microspora,* 59
Midge, 104
Milk Cap, 61
Mill Leat, 106
Millipedes, 120
Minquiers, 1
*Mnium,* 64
Mole, x, 130
Mole-cricket, 117
Molluscs, 80
*Monodonta,* 97
Mont Touraille, 21
Montague's Seasnail, 101
Moorhen, 125
Morrel, Common, 61
Mosquito, 104
Moss, Catherine's, 64
Mossy Stonecrop, 69

Moths. list of common, 116
    photos of, **38**, **39**
Moulin Huet Bay, 7, 16
Mouse, Field, x, 131
    House, x, 130
    Long-tailed Field, 131
    Striped Field, 131
    Wood, x, 131
Mullet, Thick-lipped Grey, 100
Mushroom, Common Inkcap, 60
    Field, 60
    Horse, 60
    Oyster, 61
    Parasol, **42**, 60
    Shaggy Inkcap, 60
    Shaggy Parasol, 60
    The Prince, 60
Mushrooms, 60
Mussel, Common, 99
    freshwater, 106
    Pea, 106
Mustard, Hoary, 69
Myxophyceae, 59

# N
Nannels, The, 9, 19
National Trust of Guernsey, 139
National Trust Reserve, 18
Needle shell, 97
Nematodes, 103
Neolithic Dolmens, 18
    monuments, 13
    tombs, 49
Neustria, 49
New Zealand Cabbage Palm, 71
    Flax, 71
Newt, Smooth, 108
Nine Healing Herbs, ii
Nipplewort, viii
Nit-grass, 72
Noxious Weeds Law 1933, 135
Nunnery, The, 32, 106

# O
Oak, Evergreen, 119
Oarweed, 57
    Japanese, 58

*Obelia*, 76
Obit fund, 50
*Ocenebra*, 98
Octopus, Common, 99
*Olearia*, 73
Onions, Stinking, viii
*Onopordum*, 69
*Opiothrix*, 78
Orache, Babington's, 58
    Spear-leaved, 58
Orange Peel Fungus, **42**, 62
*Orchestria*, 79
Orchid, Bee, 72, **91**
    Common Spotted, 72
    Green-winged, 72, **90**
    Heath Spotted, 72
    Loose-flowered, 72, **92**
    Pyramidal, 72, **90**, **143**
    Southern Marsh, 72
Ormer, **37**, 75, 98
*Ornithogallum*, 70
*Orobanche*, 68
Ortac, 9, 19, 123
*Orthotrichum*, 64
*Ostrea*, 99
Owl, Barn, 121, 124
    Snowy, 124
Oyster, American, 99
    Edible, 99
    Portuguese, 99
Oyster Drill, 98

# P

Paddleworm, 77
*Padina*, **48**
*Palaemon*, 80
*Palaemonetes*, 80
Pansy, Dwarf, 68
Paradis, 29
*Paramecium*, 103
Parazoa, 103
*Parmelia*, 62
Passage au Singe, Le, 19
*Patella*, 97
*Patina*, 97
Peacock, 126

Peacock's Tail, **48**, 57
Peacock Worm, 77
Peat, 7, 9, 30, 31
*Pelvetia*, 56
Pennywort, Marsh, **84**
Perch, 106
Peregrine Falcon, 121, 126
Perelle, 7
Perelle Bay, 17
Perigord Truffle, 61
Periwinkle, Flat, 97
    Rough, 97
    Round, 97
    Small, 97
*Petasites*, 72
Petit Bot Bay, 16
Petit Val, Le, 20
Petite Blaye, La, 23
Petite Monceaux, La, 27
Petrel, Storm, 123
*Phalaris*, 71
Pheasant, 126
    Golden, 126
Picaterre Farm, viii, 126
Picrite, 9
Pilcher Monument, 24
Pimpernel, Yellow, 72
Pine, Monterey, 66
Pink, Deptford, 72
Pipefish, 100
    Greater, 101
    Lesser, 101
    Worm, 101
Pipistrelle, 131
*Placynthium*, 63
Plaice, 100
Plaiderie, La, 32, 52
Planarians, 103
Plankton, 75
Plantain, Buck's-horn, ii, 58
    Sea, 72
Platte Côtil, 9
Platte Saline, 9, **14**, 19, 20, 23, 106, 115, 130, 131, 142
Platte Saline pond, ix, 20, 126, 132

Platyhelminthes, 103
Pleinmont, 7, 16
*Pleurococcus*, 59
Plover, Grey, 121
    Ringed, 121
Pochard, 124
Point Robert Lighthouse, 25
Point Sauzebourge, 26
Pollack, 102
*Polycarpon*, 67
*Polyides*, 57
Polypody, Common, 65
*Polysiphonia*, 56
*Polytrichum*, 64
*Pomatoceros*, 78
Pond Skater, 104
Poppy, x
*Porcellana*, 80
*Porphyridium*, 59
Porphyritic microdiorite, 12
    microgranite, 9
Porpoise, 102
Port du Moulin, 25
    Soif, 17
Pot Bay, 12, 25
Prawn, 80
    Chamaeleon, 80
Preservation of Natural Beauties and Prevention of Unsightly Buildings Law, 1936, 139
Prickly Saltwort, 58
Promontory forts, 31
*Protococcus*, 59
Protozoa, 103
Puffball, 60
    Giant, **41**, 60
Puffin, xi, 26, 100, 122, 123
*Punctaria*, 57

# Q

Quaking-grass, 71
    Great, 71
    Lesser, 71
Quartz, 9
Quaternary Period, 1

Quesnard Point, 138
Quillwort, Land, 65, **83**

# R
Rabbit, Black, x
Rabbits, x, 129, 130
Race, 19, 138
Radiation pollution, 138
Radon levels, 139, 140
Ragworm, 77
Ragwort, 135
Raised beach, 1, 31
*Ramalina,* 62
Ramsons, 70
Rat, Black, x, 130
    Brown, x, 130
Raven, 124
Raz Blanchard, Le, 19
Raz Island, ix
Razor Shells, 98
Razorbill, 123
Red Deer, 131
Redshank, 121
Redstart, 125
Redwing, 125
Reedmace, 109
    Lesser, 71
Reptiles, 108
Restharrow, 68
    Small, 67, **84**
Richard I, Duke of Normandy, 49
Richard II, Duke of Normandy, 50
Roach, 106
Robin, 124
Robin's Pincushions, 119
Roc à L'Epine, 30
Rock-rose, Annual, **82**
Rock Worm, 77
Rockling, Five-bearded, 102
    Shore, 102
Rocquaine Bay, 16
Rollo, 49
Roman occupation, 32
    shipwreck, 32
*Romulea,* 70
Rook, 124

Rose, Burnet, **89**
Rose Farm, 19
    valley, 125
Roselle Point, 31
Rosière Quarry, 26, 138
    steps, 26
Rosemary, ii
Rotifers, 103
Rouettes de faïteaux, 30
Roundworms, 103
Royal Alderney Agricultural
    Society, 128
RSPB, 133
Rudd, 106
Rue, ii
Rush, Dwarf, 70
    Saltmarsh, 72
*Russula,* 60

# S
Saccharina, 58
Sage, ii
Saint's Bay, 7, 16
Saline Bay, 66
Samphire, Golden, **85**
Sand-eel, Greater, 100
    Lesser, 100
Sand-hoppers, 79
Sand Cat's-tail, 71
    Couch, 58, 143
    Mason, 77
Sanderling, 121
Sandhill Snail, **35**
Sandstone, ix, 9
*Sargassum,* 58
Sark, 2, 30, 55
    Hoard, 32
    Pond, **109**
Sarkstone, 12
Saye Bay, 9
Scarlet Hood, 62
*Schistidium,* 64
*Scleroderma,* 61
Scurvy-grass, Common, 69
    Danish, 69
Sea-Couch, 58

Sea-slug, 98
    Common Grey, 98
Sea Anemone, 12, 24
    Beadlet, **46**, 76
    Snakelocks, 76
    Stalked, **36**
    Trumpet, 76
Sea Beet, 58
    Belt, 57
    Bindweed, 58, 143
    Bootlace, 57
    Couch, 143
    Cucumber, 78
    Hare, **36**, 98
    Hen, 101
    Holly, 110, 143
    Kale, 58, 110, 142
    Lemon, 98
    Lettuce, 56, 58
    mats, **45**, 77
    Milkwort, 72
    Mouse, 77
    Oak, 57
    Pea, 72
    Potato, 78
    Purslane, 67
    Rocket, 58, 142
    Sandwort, 58, 142
    Slater, 79
    Spurge, 58, 142
    Squirts, 75
    Stock, ii, 68
    Stock, Great, 68
    Thong, **48**
Sea Urchin, 28
    Edible, 78
    Green, 78
    Rock, 78
Seawater temperature, 55
Seablite, Common, 72
Seal, Grey, 102
Sedge, Sand, 58, 143
Segmented Worms, 104
Seigneurie, Sark, 24
*Semibalanus,* 79
Serin, 122

*Serpula*, 78
Shag, **92**, 122
Shanny, 100
Sharks, Basking, 99
Shelduck, 124
Shell Beach, Herm, 12, 27, 142
Shieldbugs, 119
Shingle Bank, The, 17
Shrew, x
    Greater White-toothed, 131, 132
    Lesser White-toothed, 131
Shrimp, Freshwater, 104
    Ghost, 80
    Sand, 80
Silbe Nature Reserve, 17
Silver, 12
Silver-lead, 13
Silver-leaf Fungus, 62
Silver mines, Sark, 25
Silverfish, 119
Sites of Nature Conservation Importance, 139
Slow-worm, 108
Slug, Dusky, 111
    Garden, 111
    Large Black, **35**, 111
    Sowerby's, 111
Smelt, Sand, 101
Snail, Banded, 110
    Brown-lipped, 110
    Chrysalis, 110
    Garden, 110
    Garlic, 110
    Great Pond, 105
    Hairy, 110
    Laver Spire, 105
    Liver Fluke, 105
    Marsh, 105
    Pellucid Glass, 110
    Pfeiffer's Amber, 105
    Pointed, 110
    Ram's Horn, 105
    Salt Marsh, 105
    Sandhill, 110, 143
    Slippery Moss, 110

Spire, 105
Wandering Pond, 105
Snake, Grass, 108
Snipe, 126
Société Guernesiaise, La, iii, v, 64, 112, 121, 133, 139
Société Jersiaise, The, 146
Société Serquiaise, La, iii, 133
Sole, 100
Sow-thistle, Corn, x
Sparrow Hawk, 126
Spider, Crab, 120
    Garden, 120
    House, 120
    Orb-web, 120
    Wolf, 120
Spiders, 120
Spindle-tree, Japanese, 73
Spire shell, 97
*Spirogyra*, 59
*Spirorbis*, 78
Spleenwort, Black, 65
    Guernsey, 65
    Lanceolate, 65
    Sea, 65
Sponge, Pond, 103
    River, 103
Sponges, 75
*Spongomorpha*, 57
Spotted Rock-rose, 67
Spring Starflower, 70
Springtails, 119
Spurge, Purple, 66
    Wood, 68
Squashbugs, 119
Squid, 98
Squill, Autumn, 70
St. Aman's Cup, 61
St. Andrew, 18
St. John's-wort, Flax-leaved, 67, **86**
St. Magloire, 49
St. Peter-in-the-Wood, (Parish), 132
St. Peter Port, 15, 18
St. Pierre du Bois, 132

St. Sampson, 18
St. Sampson's bridge, 15
St. Saviour, 18
St. Saviour's Reservoir, 106, 124, 132
St. Tugual, 27
Stamps, Alderney, 134
Stamps Guernsey, 134
Star-of-Bethlehem, 70
    Guernsey, 70, **85**
Star Ascidians, 76
Starfish, Common, 78
Starling, 124
Stickleback, 106
    Fifteen-spined, 101
Stinking Onions, 70
Stoat, x, 128
Stone Quarrying, 13
Stonechat, 122, 124
Stonecrop, Biting, 23
    English, 23
Stoneworts, 72
Storm Petrel, 121
Strawberry, Beach, 72
Sucker, Cornish, 101
    Lump, 101
Summer Snowflake, 70
Swallow, 124
Swan, Black, 123, 126
    Mute, 123
Swift, 124
Swinge, The, 19, 22
Sycamore, 74

# T

Talbot Valley, 18
*Talitrus*, 79
Tamarisk, 74
Teal, 124
Teasel, Wild, 72
Telegraph Bay, 22
Tench, 106
Tern, Common, 122
    Sandwich, 121
*Theba*, **35**, 110
Theophrastus, i, 80

Thistle, Cotton, 69, **89**
    Rough Star, viii
    Scotch, 69
Thistles, 135
Thongweed, 57
Thrips, 119
Thrush, 124
Tidal range, 19
Tit, Blue, 125
    Great, 125
Toad, 108
Toadflax, Bastard, 67, **81**
Toadstool, Fairy-ring, 60
Topshell, Flat, 97
    Grey, 97
    Large, 97
    Painted, 97
    Purple, 97
    Thick, 97
*Tortella*, 64
*Tortula*, 64
Tourgis Point, **143**
Treaty of St. Claire-sur-Epte, 49
Treecreeper, Short-toed, 122
Trepied Dolmen, 17
*Trifolium*, 68
*Tristagma*, 70
*Trivia*, 97
Trout, Brown, 106
    Rainbow, 106
Tubeworms, 78
*Tulostoma*, **40**, 62
Turnstone, 121

# U
*Ulmus*, 74
*Umbilicaria*, 62
*Usnea*, 63

# V
Val, Le, 21
Val Reuters, Le, 21
Val Vert Courtil, Le, 21
Vale Island, xii, 15, 18
    Pond, 18, 105, 122, 132
Vallée, Le, 21

Vallée des Trois Vaux, La, 22
Varde, La, 29
Vascular Plants, 64
Vau Pommier, Le, 22
Vazon Bay, 7, 17
    peat, 74
Velvet Shank, 62
Venus Pool, 24
*Verrucaria*, 62
Vervain, ii
*Vespula*, 118
Vetch, Bithynian, 67
Vicheries, Les, 122
Victor Hugo's Cave, 23
Vikings, 49
Vineries, 17, 18
*Viola*, 68
Violet, Dog, 68
Viper's Buglos, 73
Vole, Bank, x, 131
    Field, 131
    Water, 131
*Volucella*, 119
*Volvox*, 59
Vraic, 54, 135

# W
Wagtail, Grey, 125
    Pied, 125
    White, 125
    Yellow, 125
Wall-rue, 65
Wall Pepper, 23
Wallaby, 131
Warbler, Cetti's, 121
    Dartford, 121, 124
Wasp, Sand-digger, 118
Wasps, 112, 118
Water Beetles, 104
    Boatman, 104
    Bugs, 104
    Cricket, 104
    Crowfoot, 125
    Lanes, 21
    Louse, 104
    Measurer, 104

Mite, 105
Rail, 125
Spider, 105
Watermill, 19
    Farm, 126
Weasel, x, 128
Weather, 144
Weever, Lesser, 101
Weevil, 119
Whale, Minke, 102
    Pilot, 102
    Sowerby's, 102
    White, 102
Whelk, 98
White House Hotel, Herm, 27
Whitefly, 119
Wigeon, 124
William Longsword, 49
Winkle, Edible, 97
    Sting, 98
    Toothed, 97
Wood Blewit, 60
Woodcock, 126
Woodlice, 120
World Wide Fund for Nature, 134
World Wildlife Fund, 134
Wormwood, ii
Wrack, Bladder, 56
    Channelled, **47**, 56
    Knotted, 56
    Spiral, 56
    Toothed, 56
Wrasse, 102
    Ballan, 102
Wren, 124

# X
*Xanthoria*, 63
Xenolith, 9, 12

# Y
Yellow Horned-poppy, 143

# Z
Zig-Zag, 115
*Zostera*, 58, 79
*Zygnema*, 59